MUSINGS ALONG THE WAY

A WOMAN'S EXPERIENCES ON THE CAMINO

D1316873

ROBIN BLAIR

Published through OPUS
Located at:

5015 Connecticut Ave. NW
Washington, DC 20008
www.politics-prose.com / / (202) 364-1919

For my husband, Bill, who has supported me in all the things that sustain me. He remained steadfast before, during, and after my pilgrimage.

In the Beginning...

Children play games, and sometimes those games can set a direction for an entire life. That was the case for me. A simple game created one Thanksgiving Day culminated in a 500-mile walk across Spain on the Camino de Santiago de Compostela.

On that particular Thanksgiving Day, my four friends and I, probably ages six or seven, were playing in a vacant lot where a new house was in the early stages of construction. Many of the pine trees were still left standing, and stacks of lumber had been placed strategically around the lot. At one spot, we found a small, raised mound. We arranged for four of us to sit, as if in a "church pew," while I stood behind the mound, as if at a "pulpit."

Initially, as I recall, I was some sort of "priest" giving a sermon, possibly, and, in keeping with the holiday, on the subject of being thankful. (I might add that in all my years of raising and working with children, I do not once recall seeing any of them play "church.")

After the "sermon," the five of us lined up in single file and then, in complete silence and in a ritualized fashion, proceeded solemnly around the perimeter of the lot. That was it, and that was the game for that day, but it was not the end of the story. While we walked, I began to sense some sort of internal shift as if a kind of electricity were moving through my body. I had an eerie sense that something out of the ordinary was occurring. It was as if some sort of switch was being turned on within me, and I was left with a strange new awareness that there was more to life than what I could see or hear. But what? And why? That single sensation on that particular day has propelled me along a path as a spiritual seeker.

When the procession was over, I ran all the way home and found my mother in the backyard hanging up laundry—even on Thanksgiving Day. In my excitement, I tried to explain about the "church," and the "sermon," and, most important, the "procession." My words were insufficient in conveying the significance of what had happened. The only thing of which I was certain, and I was dead certain of this, was that something I couldn't explain, but something very real, had transpired in that vacant lot. For the rest of my life, I have more or less been on a search for what I have come to call "The Big Spirit"—the transformative mystical experience—even when I could not articulate it to myself or others.

PART ONE

Before I Left...

Years ago, my husband, Bill, and I were bemoaning the fact that he had never been to Europe. We often found ourselves fantasizing and strategizing "as if" we might get there one day; to France, in particular.

In spite of the obstacles (little money and three children), our talking and strategizing soon began to take root, and we found ourselves announcing, in specific terms, that we were going to France the following summer, for one week while the kids were in camp. We were soon getting hotel and café advice, books on France, and a generous check from Bill's parents. Finally, with the tiniest bit of extra effort, we had dates, money, and plane tickets; and, to our delight, that summer we enjoyed a wonderful week in France.

We began to refer to this sort of decision making as "the French Method." Simply put, you define a goal and then work backwards from the goal to make it happen. What you do *not* do is let obstacles deter you from achieving your goal. "The French Method" had gotten us a safari in South Africa; a new kitchen; through my exam for my counseling license; and various trips.

It was, therefore, not such a strange thing for me to announce to family and friends that I was going on a pilgrimage that entailed my walking the five-hundred-mile Camino de Santiago in northern Spain—before I had the slightest clue about how I would do it.

For years, I have been drawn to spiritual experiences and study. I have taken classes in metaphysics and Past Life Regression Therapy. I have regressed others, been regressed, and visited psychics and mediums. I have attended conferences on spiritual topics, kept a dream journal, and read countless books on spirituality, among which was Shirley MacLaine's account of walking the Camino and encountering many spiritual experiences along her way. Walking the Camino seemed like a next "logical" step for me.

At a wedding, I met a woman who had walked the Camino alone at age sixty-five, just as Shirley MacLaine had done. She told me that other than having children, it was the single most important thing she had done in her life. In true French Method style, more information, stories, and books flowed my way in support of this decision.

In the winter of 2009, my mother died. I was no stranger to death, but was unprepared for the depth of my sadness and confusion over the loss of my last parent.

During that same year, I retired from my job as an elementary school counselor. While I loved my job, it was time (Bill had already retired), and we had hoped to do some traveling.

Finally, early that April I turned sixty-four.

Death, retirement, and aging—a perfect storm, a trifecta—for something huge, profound, and memorable. A pilgrimage on the Camino would mark all three events in a significant way while feeding my continuing spiritual search.

As I considered this decision, I decided that I needed to do it soon. If I postponed it too long, it just might not happen. Therefore, that spring I began announcing—really, really announcing with all the certainty I could muster—that next spring when I turned sixty-five, to punctuate retirement and the death of my mother, I was going to walk five hundred miles alone across Spain.

I am a planner, and am fairly disciplined about adhering to whatever plan I have created. What I did not yet know, but would discover on the Camino, was the lesson of releasing the plan when it was not working. But I had to at least start with a plan, and figure out equipment, training, travel details, and finally really answer why I was doing this. Bit by bit, chunk by chunk, much like a five-hundred-mile pilgrimage, I'd be ready to leave on April 23rd of the following year.

I planned all the stuff I'd need to take, but my only interest was that it not weigh more than fifteen pounds. Bill and a knowledgeable L.L. Bean employee helped in this regard, and I was soon in possession of waterproof hiking boots, three pair of hiking pants with zip-off bottoms for hot days, three sunscreen shirts, a floppy hat, backpack, disgusting black pajamas (for sleeping in coed *albergues*), toiletries, and the tiniest, thinnest little towel I'd ever seen (and could not imagine being dried by). Done—checked.

Next, I worked on my training schedule for daily walks around Alexandria. I knew that by the time I left, I needed to be walking four or five hours a day while carrying my backpack. Libraries and gas stations helped with my endless need for a bathroom. As predicted, walking for extended periods of time produced great mental clarity. Maybe it was the endorphins or being away from other distractions, but whatever the reason, the happy results were real. Nature seemed more vivid, I was more aware of my surroundings, and I already seemed to be learning lessons and gaining insights about compassion, just by walking. So this was what it might be like to be a pilgrim.

After my plane tickets, cellphone, camera, and medical insurance were purchased, along with all my equipment and supplies, I thought that my growing anxiety about the trip would be reduced. But I thought wrong. It seemed like my anxiety grew almost daily. Why was I doing this? How would Bill and I deal with this separation? What if something happened to me? Or to someone in the family? My fears did not help Bill's and my growing separation anxiety, an old friend of our marriage. Our separations had been infrequent, but whenever they had occurred, we'd be deep into some ridiculous fight over some trumped-up issue, when, for the umpteenth time, we'd realize again that we were anxious about being separated.

As the day of departure grew near, I enjoyed several parting events: dinner with my yoga friends, dinner with our two couple friends, and a sweet good-bye dinner with Bill. I spoke to each of our three boys; I left massive lists for Bill regarding watering plants, buying and fixing meals, and paying bills. Even my dreams pointed in the direction of supporting this trip: In one, I dreamed of a funnel with water pouring (many paths becoming one or perhaps religions or races becoming one). In another, I dreamed of a stately building (the cathedral, perhaps) and a dove (the peace that might come from the walk?). Finally, on the night before I left, I dreamed that I was writing a paper on transition titled, "You Are Nowhere—Suspended in Between for a While Before You Touch Down." The messages seemed clear.

However, the night before I left, while lying in bed trying to tamp down my butterflies, I wondered why, really, I was doing this. Aren't we all spiritual beings trying to answer the two big questions: "Why are we here?" and "Where do we go when we die?" Did I have to go on a pilgrimage halfway around the world to get some clarity on these questions? Weren't there tons of other ways to remember my mother, mark my retirement, and acknowledge that I was getting older? People did this all the time, and most of them certainly didn't have to go on a pilgrimage to answer the questions.

As I continued pondering, why I was doing this became clearer. In fact, I had been working on this for most of my life. There are numerous stories of mystical experiences and heightened awareness occurring on the Camino. I knew that I longed and ached to be irrevocably touched in a mystical way. And, if I didn't actually encounter the Big Spirit on the Camino, I was at least putting myself in the best possible place for it to happen. I knew I wanted to be spiritually touched, but why? Who did I think I was? These two thoughts would be my constant companions throughout the next five weeks as I walked this ancient pilgrim route.

DAY 1

April 24, 2010

St. Jean Pied de Port to Orisson

Yesterday my driver had brought me from San Sebastian to St. Jean Pied de Port, a small French town on the French–Spanish border. The irony was not lost on me that a pilgrimage of 500 miles began with my own private driver. I was staying at the *albergue* L'Esprit du Chemin, where I had reserved a bed for the first night. Since reserved beds were not at all typical on the Camino, having this first one secured brought extra comfort to me.

The Camino has multiple routes heading toward Santiago in western Spain. I would be walking the Camino Frances, which starts in St. Jean Pied de Port and continues over the Pyrenees into northern Spain.

I checked in and was shown to a small, clean dorm room with eight bunk beds. On my bed was a note with my name and a hand-drawn scallop shell—the symbol of the Camino—and a little welcoming treat: a piece of candy. The scallop shell has several myths associated with the Camino, and is painted on guideposts and sidewalks to serve as waymarkers guiding pilgrims to Santiago. Most pilgrims also wear a scallop shell on their backpacks as they walk the path to the cathedral.

The owner of the *albergue* was warm and encouraging and, as I would come to realize in the days ahead, she had gone out of her way to make this place a welcoming home of sorts. It was slowly beginning to dawn on me that every single night would bring a new experience. Where was the bathroom? How was laundry done here? Where was my bed? These questions would need to be answered every single night. Then I recalled from my reading that a pilgrim—a "*peregrino*" like me—would come to appreciate even the tiniest effort to make an *albergue* seem like a home. I had traveled alone before as a young, single woman, spending a month in England, France, and Spain. But this felt different. I was not only alone, but I was going to be walking daily, carrying all my belongings, without any advance reservations. And I was no longer a young woman, but an older woman of sixty-five! To say that I was both exhilarated and terrified would be an understatement of my feelings. Among all this initial excitement it was sinking in: I was alone, and I would be alone for quite a while. Who did I think I was? Why was I doing this?

After settling in, I explored this lovely medieval town and managed to get an email out to Bill:

> "I am in heaven. I've just had lunch in a medieval spot with brick walls and Basque linens (oatmeal color with bold, colorful

stripes), a bowl of thick, rich seafood stew, homemade bread, red wine from a small pottery jug, while Russian and Mexican music played - go figure. Everything and everywhere is about pilgrims. We are embraced here. Staffs, scallop shells, wide hats, and lovely, lovely people. Everyone loves pilgrims and wants to help them. Maybe we should move to SJPP. Look at the mountains, help in the pilgrim office, and have stew for lunch. I know, I know. I haven't even started walking. I am so happy. Thank you for being so supportive. Love, Robin PS—no Portuguese doctors, but lots of skinny, gray-haired Germans."

I knew I was in full-blown honeymoon mode as I bought my Credencial del Peregrino—my pilgrim passport that would be stamped nightly at each *albergue*, and finally in Santiago as proof of my pilgrimage. Anyway, don't honeymoons serve the purpose of providing the blissful energy needed for launching us on a path we might otherwise be too fearful to manage on our own?

Other pilgrims began arriving at the *albergue* in the late afternoon. I met overweight Cindy from Canada who was actually planning to take a taxi over the Pyrenees. I met two young German women who had been walking the Camino in two-week chunks over several years as their vacation time permitted. I met Dutch, Brazilian, and French pilgrims, but no other Americans. This was where I first met Margarite, with her brilliant smile, cropped hair, and thin, tan body. She came in with Christian, with whom she had been walking for the past month. Walking for a month! It was hard to imagine. As we easily chatted I felt as though I had made a good friend in a matter of moments, a phenomenon which would happen over and over on the Camino.

Before dinner, the owner of the *albergue* gathered us all in the small dining room, motioned for all of us to sit in a circle, and asked that we introduce ourselves and state why we were walking the Camino. After we had shared our short stories, we all toasted each other and our pilgrimages with small glasses of port. We pilgrims spoke of our desires to mark a certain life event, to break up a stale life routine, to search for adventure, or to search for spiritual illumination. I loved this ritual, and added it to my growing collection of ceremonies blessing my pilgrimage.

A dinner of stew, bread, salad, and pudding was served to us by volunteers. At the table I sat across from a German professor who had already been walking for a while. He quickly picked up on my anxiety about the pilgrimage, and cautioned me to relax as he had learned to do. Seriously! Relax? Take an already anxious older woman, who would be walking up to fifteen miles a day, carrying all her belongings, staying in a different place each night, away from all familiar things and people, for five weeks and there would be NO RELAXING! Still, I made note of his advice. I was bringing with me my favorite quote from *The Art of Racing in the Rain:* "What is before you is what you have manifested." This notion of creating my life with the experiences met on any given day was a constant companion during my walk. Maybe I was already manifesting a need for advice about relaxing.

Bedtime was early, and most people seemed more than ready to retire. My first night of Camino sleeping would entail eight men and women in bunk beds in the same room with everyone undressing in full view of all—boxers, bras, bikini underwear. Oh, Lord.

Typically and predictably, I had a hell of a time falling asleep. It was not just my excitement and anxiety, but my multiple trips to the bathroom. It was probably (I'm guessing, here) two or three a.m. before I actually fell asleep. Lessons were pouring in. Suck it up. Deal. Keep your wits about you. Learn from others.

On the actual day of starting my pilgrimage, April 24, Margarite and I, having decided to walk together, headed down the main street of St. Jean, walked over the bridge and up onto the path that would lead us over the Pyrenees. We were on the Route de Napoleon, the exact one used by Napoleon and his army, and said to be one of the most difficult portions of the entire pilgrimage. The day could not have been more spectacular (though this was not always the case), with clear blue skies, birds singing, and the sounds of cow bells in the distance. I read all these signs as good omens for my journey.

Margarite and I continued to walk straight up the mountain, each step becoming harder as I became more winded. The path seemed to go directly up, and I was surprised at how difficult it was. Why? In my naiveté I had thought, "How hard could this be?" As it turned out, really, really hard.

Margarite began her habit of giving me advice, a habit that would continue during our coming days of walking together. Her constant instruction would come to irritate me, but for now I was grateful for information and advice from such an experienced pilgrim (she had just walked here from Le Puy, France). She told me I needed to take small steps when walking up a steep incline. She said the long strides "so typical of Americans" increased the likelihood of injury. She was patient with my many requests to stop and rest. She told me how to tell the difference between the French waymarkers (red equal signs) and the Spanish ones (yellow arrows or scallop shells), she helped me adjust my pack to reduce exhaustion, and finally, she told me the best way to manage my hiking stick. Hadn't I already known those things? I guessed not.

Along the way, we met Irish pilgrims and an East German mother and her adult son; we were given strawberries by French pilgrims; and shared mints and sandwiches with others. I was a pilgrim. Just like all the books I had read, I was now a helpful, nice pilgrim, sharing what I had with others on a beautiful day with stunning views of the Pyrenees around us.

We arrived at the *albergue* at Orisson, about halfway up the climb over the Pyrenees. Despite my original plan, Margarite had advised me to break up the walk over the Pyrenees into two days. This was to avoid an early injury, and because this portion of the walk was so taxing. My plan had been to make it over in one day in order to finish the full 500 miles by late May when I was meeting Bill in Santiago. At first I resisted changing, but that little quiet voice in my head urged me not to be stubborn and to pay attention to this advice from experienced pilgrims. It would turn out to be excellent advice, and I was grateful for not being too rigid early on the walk. This morning we had heard that there had been no beds available at Orisson (one of the few places where beds could be reserved), but just as we arrived two miraculously became available. Margarite said our Camino angels were hard at work on our behalf. I believed her! We checked in with the mother and son from East Germany, Martina and Greg, with whom we had already become friendly.

I managed a short coin-operated shower that lasted for only five minutes. I was already learning about conservation of water, soap, and shampoo. I washed my clothes from the day's long hike, and hung them in the sun to dry. Martina, Greg, Margarite, and I met on the massive observation deck, ordered cold beers, and marveled at the views of the Pyrenees. Was I really here, doing this, actually looking at the Pyrenees that I had just climbed?

With Greg and Margarite translating, we enjoyed a wonderful conversation about economics (Martina worked in a bank), the Camino (all of our longstanding desires to do this), politics (Martina's and Greg's passion for freedom), and, finally, names—and specifically the names of all our children. They all not only thought my name Robin was strange (which I really didn't understand), but the names of my children were strange to them as well. I explained that our three sons, Macon, Brooke, and Will had family names, that we were Southern, and that in the South, names can often be used for both genders, and last names were often used as first names. None of it made sense to them, but the lasting result of the conversation was that Margarite began to refer to me as "the sudren girl," and throughout our walking together for the next week would admonish me for being too accommodating (too "sudren") when I should be more direct—and Dutch! I later managed a phone call to Bill, and rattled on about the trip over, St. Jean, the wonderful people I was meeting, and the long, hard slog up the mountain. I was already missing him terribly. How would I get through almost five more weeks?

Our communal meal was enjoyed in a large, camp-like dining room. The meal was not memorable, but the people I met were. I met the German professor who had walked the Camino before. He told us how muscular we would all be at the end of our pilgrimage. I met the Irish girl who had also done this before, but had only negative observations to report. I wondered why she was doing this walk again, and made a mental note to avoid that kind of negativity. It was way too draining. And, finally, I met the middle-aged German couple, with their pressed shorts and neatly folded socks, and asked why they were here. The husband typed into the translation app on his iPhone, "I am so happy here," and beamed.

As the sun was setting, we made our way to our bunk beds, and, unlike last night, sleep came quickly.

DAY 2

April 25, 2010

Orisson to Roncesvalles

Even though Margarite and I had been able to reserve two beds at Orisson the previous day, I was the only one to actually secure a bed. When we had arrived with Martina and Greg, the *albergue* was short one bed. Margarite offered to give up her bed, and instead enjoyed sleeping in her pup tent under the stars.

In the morning, while Margarite stayed with her drying tent, I finished my toast and coffee and prepared to head out toward Roncesvalles.

A note about the ebbing and flowing of pilgrims: There are many ways to walk the Camino and a variety of ages and nationalities of pilgrims. Some pilgrims walk for extended periods of time, and others for a few days; and, as I would learn this morning, there would be times of walking alone only to reconnect with a friend farther along the trail. There were other times of starting off with a friend (or a group of friends), and somehow, during the day, finding yourself walking all alone. It must sound crazy, but that was how it went. I don't recall issues causing this shifting throughout the day, but perhaps it was due to nothing more than individual walking rates, or a desire to be alone and reflect, or a need to connect with others and talk. Whatever the reason, it became the most ordinary thing to connect, separate, reconnect, and separate again continuously throughout any given day.

So this morning I left the *albergue* at Orisson alone and walked along the road that wound up the mountain. With a crush of other pilgrims and the sun beaming on my back, I thought how lucky I was and how easily it seemed that events were lining up to make this a perfect pilgrimage. But as I would learn daily throughout my pilgrimage, nothing remained constant on the Camino. I was shaken instantly from my reverie as the road and my path veered off into a meadow, and the sunshine was replaced with a freezing wind and misty fog all around. The waymarkers were deeply embedded in the grass and far apart, making them hard to find. What had started out as a group of pilgrims had now dwindled to just me, totally by myself again. The recent words of the *hospitaleiro* filled my head: "This can be a really dangerous stretch. Be careful. Pay attention. People have died here."

I seemed to be creeping along, but in moments, and to my surprise, Margarite appeared. I was flooded with relief not to be out there alone. The weather and people were not the only things to change. The terrain did as well. We walked for a while in the meadow, then into the woods, into snow, into knee-high fallen leaves, where we encountered a snake, and, later, clumps of frogs' eggs. I took a pee on the side of the mountain. Finally, in the late afternoon, and after meeting back up with Martina and Greg, we made it to the summit of the Pyrenees. In an effort to stay focused as a pilgrim, I had decided to limit my picture-taking to one snapshot a day; not only would this reduce the distractions of planning and actually taking pictures, but it also meant that I had to mindfully and carefully figure out what that singular daily photo might be. My one photograph on this day was of me with all my gear standing on the summit with the blue, blue sky in the background. (This photo would be part of our Christmas cards the following year. Yes! I climbed up and crossed over the Pyrenees!)

The downward slope toward Roncesvalles was as steep as the climb up had been. My knees ached, and the two middle toes on my left foot burned all the way down the mountain. On the entire Camino, I would never get a blister or a pulled muscle, but I would discover many times each day what a nuisance these two toes were. Margarite, with her never-ending medical advice, told me that I needed to keep my toes dry, "dry and hard, exactly the opposite of what Americans typically do." I started to wonder if she thought that we were all idiots. I therefore began a practice that I followed every single day, and many times during each day, of stopping at two-hour intervals and switching my wet, sweaty socks for dry ones. Margarite was, as usual, totally correct.

Roncesvalles, "The Valley of Thorns," renowned as the place where Roland, Charlemagne's nephew, met defeat, was the starting place for Spanish pilgrims and others not inclined to cross the Pyrenees.

After finally arriving, we checked into the *albergue*, an ancient stone building. This austere and dark structure would house 120 tired and weary pilgrims that night. Here, we met the young Irish woman who noted that the only pilgrims walking alone were women, and thus concluded that we were the braver sex. We met Sally (finally, an American!), who had just left her job at the Obama White House, and was walking in memory of her father before heading off to graduate school in the fall.

Margarite and I found a bunk, and began what would be our normal daily routine: do our laundry, get a shower, unpack, repack. There were ample volunteers, here, and for a few extra Euros my wash was done, folded, and returned to me—a Camino luxury.

At 6:00 p.m., Margarite and I attended the church service that welcomed the pilgrims and ritualized our send-off. The old stone of the tiny church with its familiar Christian icons transported me back to my Episcopalian roots. I was no longer thinking of waymarkers, aching toes, peeing, or thirst, but rather that I was becoming part of a great stream of travelers going back hundreds of years who had set out on this journey for some deep spiritual purpose. It usually took very little for my thinking to spin off into those realms, and it was particularly easy this evening. Maybe it was just the incense, but I was thrilled as the priest read the names of all the countries represented. "Americanos." I beamed.

After six hours of tough walking, and meeting more new pilgrims, I determined that I was more than ready for bed. I settled onto my bunk, and decided to put the Mylar blanket Bill had given me on top of my sleeping bag. He had insisted that I bring it for emergencies, because, well, "You just never know." I decided that it made too much noise to be used in the *albergues* where pilgrims were always encouraged to be mindful of others. Still, I kept it unfolded on my bunk.

I was weary and assumed that sleep would come easily. I noted how pitch dark the room had become as the sun had set. The only windows were tiny slits in the walls, but since there were no lights outside, it hardly mattered. I heard the wheezing and snoring of other exhausted pilgrims and decided that I needed to take one more trip to the bathroom before finally nodding off. I slipped out of my sleeping bag, quietly put on my crocs, and padded down the aisle of bunks and downstairs to the bathrooms. When I returned to the sleeping area, I had the sickening realization that I had no clue which bunk was mine. Total darkness and bunk beds lined each side of the wall as far as the eyes could see—if the eye could see anything, which in my case they could not. Oh, Lord. I walked toward where I thought my bunk might be, hoping to spy my pack or my boots. I could see absolutely nothing, and even if I could have seen packs and boots, they were almost all the same. I knew better than to wake anyone up, or tap anyone's shoulder. I walked back downstairs hoping for some insight. What in the hell was I going to do? Part of me did see the humor in this situation, but not for long; I was so tired and I knew I needed to sleep. Finally, I went back upstairs again, and decided to walk down the room again, only farther this time. Do not ask me why I thought this would solve anything. Walking along, I could make out the tiniest glimmer of something shiny that I had not seen before. I walked toward it and, as I got closer, the tiny glimmer grew into my bright, bright, and very shiny Mylar blanket! My Mylar blanket in case of an emergency, just as Bill had said! I hopped into my sleeping bag, pulled it up along with a blanket, happily closed my eyes, and in seconds was fast asleep.

Day 3

April 26, 2010

Roncesvalles to Zubiri

"Fernando's Hideaway" blasted over the loudspeaker. It was six a.m., and still pitch dark. One hundred and twenty pilgrims swung into action in total silence except for the sounds of packing, repacking, zipping, unzipping, folding, unfolding, refolding.

Some *albergues* provided a breakfast, some not, and some, like this one, had vending machines with a paltry choice of food to eat and disgusting coffee to drink. I munched on a tangerine and sipped my black coffee while staring at a shelf in the common area. On the shelf were a pair of gloves, a small bottle of shampoo, a half-pack of cashews, an apple, and a small bottle of sunscreen. Another pilgrim saw me staring.

"Most *albergues* have shelves like this where you leave whatever you no longer need. If others need the discarded items, they just pick them up. It's a great system—it lightens the load." *Lightens the load.* This resonated with me, and I wondered what it might be like to have such a shelf for old grievances, excessive guilt, regrets, ruminations over idiotic mistakes, unnecessary shame, and embarrassments. What if we could just unload ourselves, and really lighten our load? What if there were such a shelf where we picked up the new, the fresh, the needed insights or relationships or skills to help with our journey. We do, of course, discard the unneeded and pick up the new throughout our lives, but I loved the idea of having a shelf to look at, to actively remind us of this process. How helpful that would be! I reached into my backpack until I felt the cool, slippery Mylar blanket, pulled it out, and placed it on their shelf; not because it weighed too much (certainly not, at about an ounce), but because I felt I no longer needed it, but someone else might. I did feel lighter—by just a bit. At the turn of the millennium while at a dinner party, I had asked a friend what advice she might have for her children at this singular moment in history. "Travel light and expect trouble." Indeed.

Margarite and I walked out into the cool, sweet air just as the sun was rising. As we walked along, I thought that I could do this all day. Shortly, the two young German women whom we'd met in St. Jean walked up behind us. "Hi, Margarite and Rrrrghbeeen!" (What was the deal with my name? Had they never heard of Robin Hood, or maybe Christopher Robin, or what about the comedian, Robin Williams?) We all hugged, caught up on the progress of our pilgrimages so far, acting like old, old friends even though we had met only three days ago.

My good mood waned as the day wore on and as my toes and my entire body ached. I changed my socks as Margarite had instructed, and this time she pulled out a small container of red medicine which she told me to apply to my toes. "This is from an old Frenchman I met on the Camino who had walked it many times. This will get your toes hard," she said. Then she gave me the bottle.

"Won't you need it? Can I pay you for it?"

"You can pay it forward. I'm good at medicine. Pay forward to the next pilgrim with what you are good at."

I wondered, *What am I good at?* as I took the small bottle.

During our walk, Margarite and I talked about the state of the world and devised a plan for world peace. We figured that a night in Roncesvalles for each world leader might do the trick...sharing four toilets, talking in gestures in order to be understood, sleeping amidst the snoring of 120 fellow travelers, and leaving old hatreds and conflicts on the shelf. Margarite went further by declaring that the world leaders should then be made to walk the entire Camino. "That should do it," she said. "After 500 miles of walking, surely they could get along."

In the late afternoon, dead tired, with aching feet and shoulders, we arrived in Zubiri, a sad little town. Martina and Greg showed up at the same *albergue* as we. It was here that we met Yong from Korea, Charlotta from Germany, and Sally from the US, all young, single women. Margarite took over as the medical expert and got us all to soak our feet in freezing water. After rubbing my feet with my tiny towel, I could sense the feeling returning to them. Martina said, "Margarite is our mudder." Margarite responded that we were all each other's mudders.

After the usual washing, repacking, and even napping, we all went to find a restaurant: the three young women who had terrified their real mothers by taking off on this journey, together with two older mudders (Martina and Greg had gone off for a mother/son dinner). It was the girls' night out, and, in spite of the language challenges (and with Margarite's help at translation), we managed to talk about why we were doing this. We had all been called in some way to undertake this unusual and difficult thing—walking 500 miles while carrying all we had. The young women (like most other young people I would come to meet) were searching for self-identity and understanding. Yong said, "I find self. I find God." That pretty much summed it up for all of us.

DAY 4

April 27, 2010

Zubiri to Pamplona

It was only Day Four, but I already felt as if I needed a day off. I didn't need it off because the walking was so difficult (though it was certainly not easy), but because I needed to be alone, to reflect and to think. So much had happened in my first days that each day seemed like multiple days squeezed into one. The terrain varied from woodland to mountain to urban. The contact with people vacillated throughout each day. Sometimes I was walking alone, sometimes (mostly) with Margarite, sometimes with total strangers with whom, in a matter of moments, I felt deeply connected. I wanted time to stop, to process, and to reflect, but I was concerned that if I didn't stick to my schedule, I wouldn't be able to meet Bill in Santiago by May 25. I had to keep walking.

Margarite, Yong, and I walked together. Sally and Charlotta had peeled off, as often happened, but we'd run into them again. We were like clumps of piecrust forming a ball of dough, then separating, then reforming. Early in the day, we walked through a magical woodland setting; later through an industrial park, hardly magical; and by late afternoon we were walking through the heat with little shade. The bloom was wearing off, and I did not let myself think about how much walking was still to be done. Bit by bit, chunk by chunk, I had to stay focused on just the moment which lay in front of me.

I realized by midday that I had not eaten enough, and we had not found any stores that were open. This was not good, and I was worried that by the time we would actually reach Pamplona, I would be exhausted.

My brain was flooded with musings as the walking settled into a monotonous pattern. I thought about how small the *albergues* were, and yet they always seemed large enough to provide needed rest, safety, and shelter. I was getting used to carefully saving resources: just a bit of toilet paper, turning off the water unless I was actually using it, saving even the tiniest bits of food for later. Back in my "real life," I would never have saved a few peanuts to eat later. As careful as we all were about resources, there seemed to be an endless, bountiful supply of help and goodwill that was freely given.

I was struck by how many elderly people I saw on the Camino. I saw two seventy-five-year-old Italian women who had the totally wrong sort of hiking shoes, but seemed not to mind as they walked arm in arm along the path. I met two older French couples, the men each with long, gray ponytails. I wondered if I would have seen so many older walkers back in the states.

Yong said to me, "How old you?"

"Sixty-five."

"You no look that old." Then she told me again of her search for God, but also for a husband; someone with whom she could wake up each morning and kiss to begin the day. I made a smooching sound, and assured her that I was a pretty good matchmaker, and would be on the lookout for a mate for her. We both laughed.

I also thought about how I had not encountered any whining on the Camino. An image popped into my mind of a rock in a boot. As I clomped along, my thoughts about a rock in a boot continued to develop. On the one hand a rock in the boot early in the day could spell trouble if it were not dealt with. It was not a thing to be ignored, as even a tiny rock could produce the nastiest of blisters. I thought about small rocks as things to be dealt with early, like small relationship issues, or job challenges, or even home and car repairs; best to address these things early before they have morphed into really big problems. On the other hand, there were also small rocks in boots that were simply slight irritations that did not need the energy of confrontation. They might just be overlooked or endured, but not whined about. Every single little irritation did not need to be whined about, casting unnecessary negativity into the mix. In discussing all this with Margarite, she said, "How do you tell the difference?" Yes, that was the challenge. Perhaps age...perhaps wisdom helped.

Finally, by late afternoon, we arrived at the German-run *albergue* in Pamplona. I did reflect that I was actually in Pamplona, brought to fame for many by Ernest Hemingway's description of the running of the bulls. I didn't reflect on this for long, as I was eager for rest in one of the bunk beds covered lovingly with hand-crocheted blankets. We were greeted by Jacob, the seventy-something charming and funny *hospitaleiro*, and his sweet wife, Gudrun. I felt an instant rapport with him as he eagerly engaged us in conversation about American rock and roll bands and his three attempts to walk the Camino (finally, on his third try he actually did it). I filed that story away. Three times. Hmmm. Why would anyone do that?

I felt as though I had arrived at the home of a friend and could have spent hours chatting with him. He had other pilgrims to register so he showed us to the bunk rooms, men separated from the women. Women also had their own bathrooms. It was clear that Jacob and Gudrun understood us and our longing for touches of home and caring.

Margarite and I found our bunks, and I offered to be in the top bunk this time. Climbing up the sharp metal ladder and over the equally sharp metal sides was painful, but I was happy just to lie down before starting in on the usual afternoon ritual of laundry and unpacking my sleeping bag. I did not want conversation; I did not want people; I wanted solitude and rest. As wonderful as Margarite had been, I desperately wanted to be away from her.

After some rest, however, Margarite, Yong, and I did head into old Pamplona. I knew I should have been interested in the sights—the cathedral, the streets for the running of the bulls—but I was spent. I wanted food and sleep. The small passageways were crammed with souvenir shops that blurred together. We argued over where to eat, and finally settled on a small tapas bar.

Strolling back to the *albergue* after dinner, we chatted—endlessly, it seemed—about life, the Camino so far, and our yearnings. Once back in our little home for this day, I climbed up the painful little ladder, slid into my pajamas, and conked out.

DAY 5

April 28, 2010

Pamplona to Puenta la Reina

Jacob came into the ladies' bunk room and chirped, "*Guten Morgen. Bon jour.* Time to get up!"

I rolled over in my sleeping bag and announced that I would be sleeping in this morning, and could he please bring me a cappuccino.

"Oh, zat eeze not pozzible. Get up. Gudrun has breakfast ready."

I crawled down the painful metal steps of the bunk and walked to one of the dining rooms, still dressed in my Camino pajamas, a silky black and brown number. I had managed to brush my teeth, but that was the extent of my morning grooming. Hair sticking straight up, sleep in my eyes. A sight.

I joined a group of twenty-something German men. Gudrun poured coffee for us, and served a plate of toast and jam. I was learning that not every *albergue* offered breakfast, and it was, therefore, a real luxury to have it included. To have it *served* to us was beyond a luxury!

The coffee did its job of waking me up, and I was shortly in a conversation with these young men. "Why are you here? What has it been like so far? What do you hope to get from your experience?" The open-ended questions poured out of me. The men easily talked about their experiences, their feelings, and their hopes (they mostly wanted to shake up their lives). Part of me was connected to their conversation, but another part was observing the scene. I was halfway around the world, dressed in my pajamas, having an intimate conversation with complete strangers…young strangers…male strangers, and it didn't even seem odd.

Early in the pilgrimage, most people that I met were fairly positive. Hello, honeymoon! But one young man said that he was struck by how kind everyone on the Camino was, and that "everyone feels your pain, and they always try to help if they can." It was the first time I'd heard the word "pain." He was correct. There was definitely pain on the Camino, and people did seem to want to help. I was forming a stereotype of the pilgrims I'd met so far: They were nice, and helpful, but also open, tolerant, curious, and very smart. Additionally, they were attractive! Even as bedraggled as everyone was by the end of the day, the pilgrims I'd met were attractive. What was that about? And so far, everyone had a compelling reason for being here.

After breakfast, we packed up, and I talked briefly with the two breast cancer survivors who were walking in thanksgiving for surviving their disease. I couldn't imagine doing this after having had chemotherapy.

As we approached the door, both Jacob and Gudrun stood there wishing each of us a good and safe journey. I hugged both of them and said that

I loved them, and they returned the sentiment. Telling total strangers that I loved them? Who does that, and why was I doing that? And yet it seemed genuine and totally appropriate. What a nice way to start the day.

Margarite, Yong, and I walked through the streets of Pamplona We picked up Martina and Greg and left behind another pilgrim from the *albergue* to nurse her tendonitis. As we walked out of the city, we met another German woman, a young Korean man (not up to Yong's standards), a young American couple who were biking the Camino, and two seventy-year-old women, one an Australian and the other an American who had just retired from the IMF (International Monetary Fund). We also met a sixty-nine-year-old man from Barcelona walking for the second time and marveling at all the women he was meeting. I hardly felt like a pilgrim; more like someone at a social mixer! The day was lovely, the low mood of yesterday was gone, and I was having the time of my life and fully appreciating my good fortune.

Midday, our band of pilgrims stopped in an old churchyard to have lunch. Margarite put a handkerchief on an old bench to serve as a makeshift tablecloth. I gathered some wild flowers and put them in a water bottle. Margarite played a recording of Loreena McKennitt's "Santiago" on her phone while we spread Spanish cheese, almonds, ham, on a baguette we'd purchased on the way out of town. Others walking by joined us, including GGG (Gorgeous German Guy). As he approached, I said that we were a crazy bunch. "I zee. I like eet." We ate, talked, laughed, and enjoyed the music and sunshine. My one photo for this day was a group picture of all of us. I told everyone that I was writing a book about the Camino, but that I would change their names. "Oh, we are not like Americans. We will not sue you. You can keep our names."

After this wonderful lunch, we trudged in the hot and shadeless afternoon until we had walked ten hours, our longest day so far. My toes burned, and I switched my socks throughout the afternoon. At five p.m., we arrived at Albergue Jakue in Puenta la Reina. This was a three-star hotel with beds for pilgrims in the basement. In this basement, we had privacy screens, modern showers, and a large kitchen. After doing our wash, I hung all of our laundry out. It dried quickly in the heat.

There was a hotel buffet dinner that made us all feel that we were no longer weary, smelly pilgrims, but sophisticated women friends going out for dinner.

During our dinner of pasta, salad, and wine, followed by ice cream, we talked, as women often do, of falling in love and getting married. Each woman told her story. The younger women listened as the two old mudders told of meeting our husbands, falling in love, and getting married. "How did you know? How can you know? What was it like? And suppose it never happened?" It had been ages since I'd had a conversation about falling in love and getting married. I felt old. Wise, but old.

After dinner, as we prepared for bed, a teary Yong asked to speak to Margarite and me. She said that she had loved getting to know us and walking with us but she was hungering for some solo time to ponder her deep longings. Today, walking and talking with so many people, and having the lunch in the churchyard, had been overwhelming for her. We all hugged, and reassured her that we understood. Then she handed each of us a small gift. Maria went to her pack and also came back with a small token for each of us. I felt awkward at having nothing for them. Margarite said that my book would be the gift. *Yes, I just have to write it.*

DAY 6

April 29, 2010

Puenta la Reina to Estella

"Okay. I hate Spain. I hate the damn
Camino! I hate the graffiti and the heat. I
hate the putrid smell that we sometimes
encounter. And tonight it is raining, and I
wonder how my clothes will ever dry. And
maybe I'm getting a cold. And I have not
been able to get Bill on the phone. And my
schedule is off by a day, and I am cranky,
wondering how I will make up that day.
And I want to be alone. And, yes, I am
whining, I know, I know, after I said there
wasn't any whining on the Camino. Okay.
I was wrong."

At least that was what I wrote in my journal
sitting on my top bunk after walking eight hours
to get to this *albergue* in Estella. I knew I was
whining in my head, and that I was homesick and
that I was missing Bill, and that I was
wondering—just as my guidebook had said I
would—why on earth I was doing this?

I hadn't started the day hating the Camino or
wondering why I was doing this. I was perfectly
happy as we left Puenta la Reina with our reduced
band of pilgrims. Yong was long gone by the time
Margarite and I had even gotten up. Sally and

-44-

Charlotta left on their own. And Martina...I was not even sure where she was, except that this was Greg's last day, so perhaps a mother/son walk had been in order. I had been happy when we started out, but the heat and the eight hours of walking made that good feeling evaporate.

The day was filled, as it always was, with countless conversations: pacifism, guns and gun control, and motherhood, specifically labor and delivery. Do women ever tire of recounting and revisiting one of the most profound events of their lives? Mothers loved to talk about their pregnancies, their labors, their deliveries, and, of course, their children. The more excruciating the details of the labor and delivery, the better. Margarite and I were no different. In spite of our differences of language, age, and nationality, we found a bond over sharing the details of the births of our children. The idea of the Camino being like a mother to us was percolating in my mind.

When we arrived at the *albergue* in Estella, we were greeted by the cheery Italian *hospitaleiro*, Stephan. We did our usual post-walking activities, and then shopped for food. Later, Margarite and some other pilgrims visited the church in the town while I sat on my bunk bed writing and relishing this time alone.

Stephan fixed and served us an all-white, but very much appreciated, dinner of pasta, cheese, salad, bread, and a white pudding. I asked Stephan about my pilgrim stereotype, of pilgrims being nice, smart, and good-looking. I wondered if that had been his experience as well. "Good God, no!"

he said and told me that only this morning there had been several rude and inconsiderate pilgrims who had thoughtlessly awakened others.

At an earlier than usual time after dinner, I crawled into bed and was lulled to sleep by the rain falling on the roof.

Musings for Today:
- Litter did not exist on the Camino. Why, when there was so much graffiti?
- I met a Canadian couple today who told me about training in a Maine resort over the summer. With packs on their backs, they had been stopped by local police who thought they were homeless and had never heard of the Camino. We were certain that the Martin Sheen movie would change all that.
- I was not sure what else Margarite could teach me. Today she told me to stop looking down as I walked because my shoulders would start to hurt, and besides, it was a sign of depression. *What?* "What about the rocks I might trip over?" "Trust your feet and use 'soft' eyes, just glancing down every now and then." Once again, she was right, and even now, when I am hiking, if I look down for too long I hear her voice in my head urging me to look up. Later in the day, we talked about Edgar Cayce, the great psychic and father of the New Age. Actually, *we* weren't talking, *I* was, and it felt great to finally be able to

impart some information to her. She thanked me for being her spiritual teacher. I knew the day was coming when we would go our separate ways. I knew that happened on the Camino, and that I, like Yong, was longing for some quiet, meditative time. Just not yet.

DAY 7

April 30, 2010

Estella to Los Arcos

Blessed sleep, cool morning, good cereal—a nice start to a day that was sunny and pleasant. Margarite and I headed out through the small, historic town of Estella to be reunited with Martina. Greg had left to return to Germany. The three of us walked until we reached the Bodegas Irache, with its famed fountain offering pilgrims free red wine. As per tradition, we filled our scallop shells with the red wine, drank its sweetness, and enjoyed a photo op.

We arrived at a fork in the road: one way, the main path up to Monjardin; the other, the alternate path through the woods and pastures above the hill town of Luquin. I was craving solitude and opted for the alternate route away from our small group.

They left together, and I walked alone up the gentle woodland path. I was totally and completely alone for the next nearly four hours. My walking quickly fell into its familiar rhythm as I soaked in the scenery and peacefulness. I wasn't frightened or worried about running out of water. I was well stocked. The waymarkers led me easily and effortlessly along. While not even consciously observing the path, my thoughts went to my notions of the Big Spirit. I was aware of all the little ones that I'd already encountered: getting a bed at Orisson, receiving advice from the kind *hospitaleiros*, meeting warm and helpful fellow pilgrims. But so far the Big Spirit had been elusive—which was to say, non-existent—for me. Certainly by the end of five weeks I will have encountered the Big Spirit. This high, ancient path where I was totally alone would be the perfect setting. Wouldn't it? I was pretty sure that Big Spirit events would be hard to miss, probably knocking you over with their arrivals.

I came upon a small fork in the road and for a moment I wondered if I was still heading in the right direction. Had I strayed off the path without realizing it? Before I'd even had time to locate a waymarker—a shell or an arrow—a cyclist riding from the opposite direction looked me over and pointed to the way he'd just come. "This way." Small spirit arrived right on time. As I walked, I sipped water and ate the fruit and nuts purchased in Estella.

Eventually, I arrived at another fork in the path, actually a T-bone intersection with one path going right, the other left. I looked around for waymarkers and saw none. Without venturing on either path, I scanned the landscape for the familiar yellow signs. Nothing. The walk so far had been so smooth and effortless that I was caught off-guard at not knowing exactly which way to go. A slight chill crept up my spine. I closed my eyes.

Get a grip. You cannot go wobbly here. Keep your wits about you. Breathe in, breathe out.

I decided to turn right at the fork and walked for probably ten minutes, but still there were no waymarkers. I began talking to my dad: "Give me a sign. Something to let me know which way I should be going. Please." Nothing came. I was aware of the pounding in my heart. I knew I did not want to keep walking in a direction that might be wrong, and I certainly didn't want to get lost in the remote hills of Spain all alone.

I turned and walked back the other way, hoping to spy something that I'd missed the first time. I was soon back at the T-bone and began walking in the other direction. Within seconds, I saw not only a yellow arrow, but Christian, whom I'd met on my very first night, sitting on the side of the hill eating an apple. I was flooded with relief. We chatted for a short while, remarking on the beauty and the solitude. I sensed that he wanted more solitude, told him good-bye, and followed the path, which was now descending into the small town.

Along the way, I pondered the notion of waymarkers, and how they help in whatever journey we might be on. The actual waymarkers for pilgrims were, of course, the yellow scallop shells and yellow arrows pointing you in the correct direction. But waymarkers were now the symbol of help arriving in all its forms—pointing out directions, advice on *albergues*, help with aches and pains. It felt like there had already been an abundance of help for my pilgrimage, and that I was never really alone. But the real task was to notice the help, and to pay attention to its arrival in all its subtle forms.

By the time I had arrived in the town, I had managed a phone call to Bill, euphoric that I had maneuvered this ancient path alone on that day. Even with the heat and lack of shade, I fairly bounced along on the way into Los Arcos. It was almost May; we were soon out of Navarre, and for the first time I was sensing progress; little steps heading in the right direction.

In the late afternoon, I arrived at Albergue Austria. Margarite had arrived earlier and had wonderfully reserved a bed for me. After settling in, I went to the peaceful garden to relax, write, and reflect. There was a simple stone sculpture of a scallop shell. I fantasized about having such a sculpture in our yard or in a lake house, should we ever buy one. I wanted scallop shells everywhere.

Soon other pilgrims arrived, and among them were, of all people, Yong and GGG, the Gorgeous German Guy. We hugged, delighting in our reunion, and yet just a week ago I knew neither of them. We talked about our walk so far, and decided to fix dinner here, as this *albergue* had a well-stocked kitchen. We shopped at a local market, Margarite and I haggling over the amount of food to buy.

"I've raised three sons. I know what hungry people will eat."

"Rohbeen! That is too much food!"

"Trust me on this," I insisted.

We sat in the kitchen while two Greek men finished fixing their meal. I was intrigued that they had thought to bring heads of garlic with them on their pilgrimage.

When we finally had the kitchen for our work, I fixed what I was calling "Pasta Camino," a concoction consisting of what we had found in the local market. We cooked heaping portions of steaming pasta topped with oily tuna, avocado, tomatoes, cheese, and olive oil. We heated several French baguettes, and fixed a large green salad. Martina brought up two small pottery jugs filled with red wine. We sat at the long table with our feast filling our plates. I taught everyone what had become the Blair blessing, a pre-dinner grace that Bill had learned from a Bishop of North Carolina: "May the Lord bless us and bind us, and tie our hands behind us, and throw us in the bushes where the Devil can't find us." I was showing them appropriate accompanying hand gestures: devil horns, tied hands, etc. I was certain it made little sense, yet everyone joined in and laughed hysterically, the same reaction the blessing always brought whenever we said it before dinners with friends back in Alexandria.

To Margarite's amazement, every single bit of food was eaten, along with the chocolate bars that one of the group donated. With Margarite doing the main translation, we talked about our jobs, East and West Germany, and the profound joys of freedom. We talked about "paying it forward," which was a new concept for GGG. With that, he offered to do all the dishes to "pay it forward" and promised to continue to pay it forward for the rest of his pilgrimage. He told us that he was a divorced forty-year-old television producer, that he had felt compelled to walk the Camino, that all the signs had "just lined up," and that he felt he had to do it. That made perfect sense to us, as we had all also been called to walk.

This was a perfect night, and had been a perfect meal. I wanted to pinch myself. How had I gotten so lucky? How would I ever be able to tell Bill or others about this in such a way that they would truly understand? As seemed to happen frequently, I was part of this evening, yet at the same time I was outside of myself, observing. We were a karass, a term coined by Kurt Vonnegut. A karass was a group of people somehow bound or linked together in a cosmically significant way, fulfilling the will of God. I had always loved that idea and considered its existence long before I knew the term. I regarded my childhood group of girlfriends, "The Five Girls," a karass. During high school; at my first teaching job; and now with the women of my yoga group, I enjoyed the belonging of a karass, and felt bound by something larger than the mere members of the group. Here we also had formed a karass. After only a week in northern Spain, with aching toes and sweaty, dirty clothes, we clomped along over mixed and challenging terrain, each connected through a call to walk this old path, a way traveled by so many others who had also been called, and along the way we shared our deepest feelings and ideas.

As the night wore on, other pilgrims stopped by our table for wine, chocolate, and conversation. There was good energy here. I was filled to spilling at the end of this magical day, and knew I would remember this as one of the most treasured of the Camino.

DAY 8

May 1, 2010

Los Arcos to Logroño

There would be no middle way today. The total enchantment of last night would evaporate into exhaustion and despair by the end of this long day.

But first I needed to eat breakfast. The breakfast provided by the *albergue* was simply dark bread with jam and coffee, but as I sat with the Germans as they ate I could clearly see their excitement at the sight of this bread. Really? Plain dark bread? They explained that this was their traditional breakfast, and that it took their minds to thoughts of home. Searching for, seeking, and noticing any reminder of home occupied all of us. Their excitement over the brown bread made me think of the power of food—its smell, texture, taste, and, most important, its associations that can instantly transport each of us to another time and place. It made me remember the happy times I had spent with my father, usually in front of a winter fire, shelling pecans from our one tree. We'd been given the task of shelling enough nuts for my mother's Southern pecan pie or the bourbon-soaked pecan cake served sparingly at Christmas. Maybe it was the time spent talking with my dad, or getting his singular attention, or the coziness of the fire, but to this day the smell and taste of pecans quickly take me back to my childhood living room. I understood the Germans and was happy for their little bit of connection to the familiar.

Today's walk began with all of us dressed in our rain gear for the first time. In an effort to stick to my schedule as much as possible, Margarite and I decided to walk all the way to the college town of Logroño, a thirty-kilometer trek, and the longest so far. It would prove to be not the wisest decision. The early path, happily, was flat, yet also filled with mud which splattered all over my boots and up my pants. It gradually caked everywhere.

We walked past rock cairns that filled the meadows and made them seem like holy places. At another point, while walking past a busy highway, we passed a long line of chain-link fences filled with handcrafted crosses made of sticks, twigs, straw, or whatever material that could be found. My recent interest in numbers led me to try to calculate how many crosses there were. I scanned the number of fences I could see ahead, and then figured an average number of crosses per fence section. I quickly calculated that we were probably passing at least 4,000 crosses, an astonishing number. When I shared my calculations with Margarite, she seemed totally unimpressed, both with my mathematics wizardry and the vast number of crosses. She simply said, "You are probably right."

Pilgrims occupied their minds with the oddest things—such as calculating numbers of crosses—

or, as one pilgrim said, calculating the number of slugs (giant four-inch slugs!) along any given path. It had to have been a huge number.

Martina and Yong had stopped several villages before Logroño. It would be the last time I would see either of them. Margarite and I walked wearily over the bridge and into the town at around five thirty p.m. At the first *albergue*, we sat down for the familiar checking-in process, bone weary and eager to get to our beds. We were stunned to learn that there were no beds! I had read that this could be a possibility, but we had so far been lucky and had always managed to get a bed. To find the *albergue* full on our longest day of walking (ten hours today) seemed especially disappointing. We figured that the late check-in hour and the fact that it was a Saturday might have contributed to this unfortunate situation. Would we actually be sleeping on the sidewalk? Margarite prevailed upon the *hospitaleiro* to call another *albergue* for us. Even so, she advised us, "There won't be any reservations. You might have thought about this." In spite of her irritation with us, she did make a call, and was able to secure two beds. "If you can quickly walk across town in the next half hour, you can claim them." I hadn't imagined that I could walk any more on this day, but the thought of sleeping on the sidewalk spurred me on.

With renewed energy, we quickly walked across town and found the second *albergue*. The *hospitaleiro* in charge was rude and demanding, collecting passports from all the pilgrims. The *albergue* was one large room filled with forty beds placed in close proximity to one another. The coed bathroom, with only two toilets, was dirty, with hair all over the sinks and floor. There was a small rooftop area for drying clothes. Many of the pilgrims here did not seem like pilgrims at all, but Spanish cyclists out for a weekend adventure and sleeping in cheap quarters.

I found a top bunk and crawled up just to rest before showering or washing clothes. I was exhausted. My feet ached, my back ached, my misbehaving toes ached, and I was aware of scratchiness in my throat. I was a pretty healthy person—or at least that was what I always told myself and others—I did not get headaches or have allergies, nor did I like to focus on ill health. However, when I did get sick or when I was stressed, the symptoms always showed up in one of two places in my body: my throat or my stomach. Sensing this scratchiness in my throat was a sure sign that I was coming down with something—a cold or perhaps something worse. It had not occurred to me that I might get sick while walking on the Camino. I had expected blisters or pulled muscles, but not actual sickness. I lay on the bed, weary, feeling sorry for myself, and wondering once again why I was doing this. And who did I think I was? And missing my home and husband and all things familiar.

While I lay there, I noticed something else: Margarite going from bed to bed, asking how folks were, if there was anything she might do to help them, and did anyone want a neck or leg massage, which she "was qualified to administer." Several pilgrims took her up on her offer for a short massage. What struck me was her absolute kindness, her compassion. Hadn't she just walked for ten hours, much of it in the rain? Hadn't she just walked across town to find a bed and listened to the incredibly rude *hospitaleiro*? Wasn't she exhausted and wondering why she was here? I thought about the aspect of *noticing* as the first requirement of compassion. She was paying attention—not to her own aches, but to everyone else's. That one episode stayed with me throughout my entire time on the Camino, and has stayed with me since returning home. I thought I had understood compassion, but not until that moment did I form the idea that really noticing and paying attention to other people was the first stage of showing it.

After a short rest, I did manage a shower in the creepy and disgusting bathroom. I washed my muddy clothes and hung them on the roof to dry. The German couple from Orisson was there. At Orisson, both had pressed shorts and neatly combed hair. Now the husband slumped on his bed, bedraggled and worn. When I asked how they both were, he looked up and gestured with his hand, sweeping the room with a disgusted look on his face as if to say, "Can you believe this place?" No, I cannot!

Margarite and I went to dinner next door in the small bar where locals were watching a soccer match. We ate overcooked steak, greasy fries, and a bland tart. I hadn't imagined that we could have any more conversation in us, but surprisingly we did. We talked about mothers-in-law, crossing borders in Europe, having daughters (Margarite doing that bit of talking), social customs, and, finally, how early we planned to bolt from this *albergue* the following morning.

DAY 9

May 2, 2010

Logroño to Ventosa

At six thirty a.m., we launched ourselves from the dreadful *albergue*, stopping in a nearby park to munch on yogurt and nuts. We walked easily along the paved and flat bike path on this chilly, overcast day. There was little conversation except for Margarite's observation about organized religion: "I am not sure why I belong to a church run by silly old men. Religion is like a family, flawed and imperfect for sure, but what else do we have? Robin, you need to settle any debate about this; pick one, flawed and imperfect, and stick with it." She also shared her opinion that she thought cyclists (of which there were tons) were not actually pilgrims. Only walkers could be pilgrims because we walked with our souls. The cyclists had left their souls behind.

Fine. Whatever you think. I was not in the mood for chatter, feeling sicker with my cold than I did last night.

We were now, finally and happily, in the next region, La Rioja, whose famed vineyards produced their prized red wine. We stopped for lunch in one of the villages and ran into Christian and the young breast cancer survivor, Maria. We enjoyed a tasty quiche for lunch, which was perfect, as I was starving. Even though my plan—and Margarite's—had us walking all the way to Najera, I decided that I would walk the shorter distance to Ventosa. This early in the day, I was already feeling exhausted, and my cold was full-blown. I didn't think about my plan or my schedule. For the rest of the morning, Christian and Maria walked with us until we arrived at the hilly town of Ventosa. Albergue Santornino was not yet open, so I dropped off my pack at the front door while we went to a bar for a cup of tea.

Walking up the hill to the bar, I was aware of my mounting dread at saying good-bye to Margarite. I silently rehearsed over and over in my head exactly what I wanted to say.

We enjoyed a cup of tea, my last treat for these fellow pilgrims. I was totally distracted by my internal dialogue. Finally, with a lump forming in my throat, I stood up. I knew it was time. I didn't want to be overly dramatic, and yet it seemed that the Camino was always ripe for drama. Experiences were enhanced, and emotions were intensified. I began telling Margarite how much I treasured our week of walking together, how much I had learned from her, how much help she had provided. As I talked, the tears began to flow. She stood up, and Christian and Maria turned away as we said our good-byes. I said she had provided the perfect introduction to the Camino; that I had learned so much about compassion by watching her tend to others. She then said that she also had loved walking with me, that I had been her teacher, that whatever I lacked in directional skills I more than made up with my connections to the other pilgrims. She said that by watching me as I learned of the stories of others, she was learning how to be more open. At this point, we were both sobbing, proclaiming our love for each other. I told her that I believed my mother had sent her to watch over me. Finally, hugging and crying, we said, as if we were young girls again, that we would be friends for life. (In fact, we would never see each other again.)

Afterwards, I headed down the hill to the *albergue*, crying the whole way.

PART TWO

DAY 9
(continued)

I walked the short distance down the hill from the café to Albergue Santornino. As I headed up to the door, I saw instantly that my pack and stick were missing. Why had I so stupidly left them outside? I pounded on the door, and as it swung open, to my relief I saw my stick and pack leaning against the wall with other sticks and packs. The calm, smiling *hospitaleiro* said that pilgrim belongings were rarely taken and please come in.

After checking in, I looked around and saw a large, open room with a fire burning in the fireplace at one end. There were Spanish tiles, antiques, pottery, large overhead timbers in the ceiling, and a long wooden table with lit candles. Classical music played softly in the background. The contrast to the previous night was striking and welcome.

While other pilgrims were reading and writing, I collapsed at the table feeling numb and spent. I recalled again that the word *peregrino* (which we were all called) not only meant "pilgrim" but also "stranger." I was a stranger, a homeless orphan, moving from place to place with an entirely new "family" each night. My friends had gone, and even though my solitary situation was sinking in, I made no attempt to engage with the other pilgrims. I sat without any plans for dinner, doing laundry, or even finding a bed, letting these surroundings provide a kind of nourishment. The warmth of the simple furnishings, the smell of the fire, the music—reminding me of my father—fed me and seeped into my soul.

The *hospitaleiro* brought me steaming tea and lemon drops for my throat. Through more tears I told her that my friend was gone, that I was on my own, and that my plan of walking all the way to Santiago by May 25th was shot. I told her that my schedule was already off by two days, and I wasn't sure how I'd make them up without using some sort of transportation. She listened and then suggested that I take a bus to Burgos, several towns away. She further suggested that I stay in a hotel for several days until I felt better. She would help me with bus schedules and hotel reservations. She also was sure that I'd see my friend again, as "that is just the way things happen on the Camino." While her plan sounded so appealing, I told her that a bus ride all the way to Burgos would eliminate four days of walking. She simply said, "St. James was a pilgrim. He understands. He forgives." Even though I knew I might be altering my goal of walking all the way to Santiago, her plan was already taking root in my mind.

She then took me to a small room with several bunk beds covered in plaid spreads. She told me to lie down, and also to lay down any burdens, and just rest. I loved the otherworldly way she spoke. I was blessedly alone and slept for the next three hours.

In the late afternoon, the room filled up with other women pilgrims. I showered in the all-female bathroom, appreciating this small luxury. I washed clothes and hung them in a separate room for drying; and realized that in the last week I'd lost a pair of underpants. How on earth had that happened without my noticing? Somewhere along the Camino rested a lone pair of black undies.

Since Albergue Santornino had a small pilgrim's store on the first floor, I decided to buy some food for dinner and prepare it in the well-equipped kitchen. I was too tired to walk through the cold and wind to the village café for dinner. Also, I loved this place and did not, even for a brief period, want to leave it. I was craving vegetables, and bought peas, peppers, pasta, an apple, a bun for breakfast, and a small Santornino handkerchief, my only souvenir from the Camino. To this day when I use it in a basket of bread or crackers, I am reminded of the beauty and good will of this place.

I began preparing dinner when I noticed that a happy group of pilgrims had formed in the kitchen, another karass of sorts. I was content to eat alone, and in fact preferred it tonight. I didn't want conversation, or stories, or to learn all the reasons these people were here. I was cranky and quiet. But in spite of myself, the social pull was too strong to resist, and I was soon laughing, talking, and getting to know an entirely new group of people. I felt like the reluctant child at a birthday party, determined not to have fun, but swept into it in spite of herself.

When our separate meals were cooked, we put everything on the table, along with several bottles of Rioja wine, and shared the food. And who were we? A Frenchman; a Swiss lady; an American, John, whom I'd met two days ago and to whom I'd given a pair of earplugs; a Japanese couple (he was the architect who was here looking for inspiration for a church design); and a darling young woman, a German lawyer whose six languages provided the evening's translations.

Our conversations were simple, and funny, as we laughed about everything. I could not have predicted how much laughter I would experience this night as our camaraderie grew. At one point, someone suggested that we each teach the group our native toasts. "Cheers, *skol*, *prost*, *à votre santé*, *salute!*" I am not sure why that entertained so much.

Later that night, I called Bill and tried explaining how many different days and emotions and experiences had been packed into one brief period. I tried to help him understand this experience, this day of leaving my friend, having dinner with these strangers, and yet feeling connected and not strange at all. I told him that my original plan of walking all the way to Santiago was being aborted, but that tomorrow I'd enjoy a bit of a respite. I went to bed happy...the last thing I would have imagined.

DAY 10

May 3, 2010

Ventosa to Burgos

Gregorian chants played throughout the *albergue* as I packed up my still-damp clothes in the early morning. I did not want to leave this place, as I still ached all over and knew I'd be heading out alone. I didn't feel ready.

I said good-bye to the *hospitaleiro* and thanked her for her many kindnesses, including help with bus and hotel reservations. She smiled and said, "*Buen Camino.* Go west." Yes, but where exactly was west?

I walked through the hilly streets of Ventosa and eventually through acre after acre of the Rioja vineyards. The ten kilometers of walking was peaceful, along gentle paths with easy to follow waymarkers. I noted again that even though I had had parts of days walking alone, this was the first time that I would not be reconnecting with a familiar face at the end of the day. I enjoyed the solitude and the chance to do exactly what I wanted. I was aware that the novelty of the pilgrimage had worn off, and a kind of flatness seemed to envelop me. The red clay, while good for the grapes, soon clumped on my boots.

By late morning, I arrived in Najera—urban, noisy, grimy, my least favorite town yet. With help I found the bus station, and with even more help I deciphered the schedule. Finally, I bought my ticket to Burgos.

In the early afternoon, after sitting for several hours in the cramped station, I boarded the bus. It rolled out of the station and into the Spanish countryside. This was the first time in two and a half weeks that I had ridden anywhere. Riding a bus, such an ordinary thing, now seemed so unusual. In spite of my misgivings about riding and not walking to Burgos, I loved being on the bus, head to the window as we passed through the lush countryside.

My thoughts turned to the notion that I had become a "cheating pilgrim," not an actual one who walked the entire 800 kilometers to Santiago. I had planned everything so carefully, except for unanticipated events—such as getting a sore throat. I felt sad and disappointed with myself. At the same time, I reflected on the many different ways I'd heard of people doing this: There was the World Bank retiree who walked during the day without a pack and was met with a glass of chilled champagne by her tour van at the end of the day; then driven to her boutique hotel. And the German women who walked as far as they could during their two-week vacations, each year adding more kilometers as they inched their way to Santiago. There were my artist friends who had walked a bit in the morning, and painted in the afternoon for only several weeks (certainly not five), but who certainly felt that they had walked the Camino. In fact, by the end of my pilgrimage, I would encounter pilgrims who rode bikes, rode horses, walked only three days out from Santiago, walked half the way, or for two months coming from France. It seemed that there were as many ways to walk the Camino as there were people to do it. Even so, I still felt nearly guilty and a little sad that I was leapfrogging four days of walking by riding the bus to Burgos. But I didn't feel so guilty or sad that I couldn't fall fast asleep with the gentle rocking of the bus.

I arrived in Burgos in the afternoon, and walked the short distance to the Hotel España. The *hospitaleiro* had wisely picked a hotel close to the train station. I knew this was a city famous for its architecture, its statue of El Cid (which I did manage to see), and its stately cathedral, but my only interest was in getting to my hotel as quickly as possible. Throughout the journey, as awful as it must sound, I was always less interested in the famous sites along the way, and far more interested in the people I was encountering or a spiritual reflection I was having...or the rest that was coming.

The desk clerk, a thin, nervous man, but with such a warm smile, quickly checked me in. My room was chilly and so tiny that I had to turn sideways to maneuver around the bed. The towels were threadbare, the bar of soap small and without fragrance, and the tub a substandard size. None of this mattered. I didn't care. What mattered was that I had a private room! Just me, all by myself, all night long. I had a full bed with sheets, my own tub and my own toilet, no one snoring to keep me awake, and no one that I had to talk to. I was in heaven.

I unpacked my still-damp clothes, and laid them out to dry. I filled the tub with steaming water and added two shots of shampoo. Oh happy day! I was going to soak in a tub, all by myself. I slid into the tub, and marinated for an hour, adding hot water as needed. After my soak, I crawled into bed for a solitary two-hour nap.

After my nap, I walked to a small bar close by for an early dinner. It was freezing and extremely windy, and at the bar I learned that bad weather was predicted for the next two days. I enjoyed my dinner alone, the first time I'd eaten alone since I started the pilgrimage. This dinner reminded me of some of the solitary dinners I had enjoyed during my solo trip to Europe at age twenty-six. I thought about how these two trips bookended major turning points in my life: the first on the cusp of adulthood, and this one on the cusp of old age.

After returning to my hotel room, I was aware of how depleted I still felt. Even with the bus ride, the soak, the nap, and the meal, I was ready for bed by seven p.m. I loved the quiet sanctuary of this funny little place and slept better than I had in days.

DAY 11

May 4, 2010

Burgos to Hornillos del Camino

Even though urban walking can sometimes be challenging, I walked easily through and out of Burgos. As I walked, I had a little chat with myself: *Shape up. You have had a bus ride and a comforting hotel stay with a soak in a tub. You can do this. This will be a good day. Manifest a positive attitude. By tonight you will be one-third done!* I knew I was in my plodding sophomore year on the Camino. The bloom of freshman year had withered and junior and senior years were still beyond my reach.

I walked the several kilometers before reaching the *Meseta*, the great cereal fields of central Spain. The *Meseta* is noted for extreme weather, fields of golden grains, and a sparse population. It has also been written that there is a bit of the mystical associated with it. When I was preparing for this pilgrimage and saw pictures of the *Meseta*, I wondered how easy it might be to get lost in this immense sea of grain.

As it turned out, walking on the very flat *Meseta*, with its single, easily followed path, was relatively easy to manage. What was not easy to manage was the wind. It felt to me that the temperature must be close 32° F and the winds at least fifty miles per hour. At home, any winds this strong would have blown down our outside umbrella and tossed things off our deck. Several times, I literally struggled to remain upright. I was so glad that I had brought light gloves and an extra blue fleece vest.

There was only the barest sprinkling of other pilgrims walking on this stretch. As I walked, my thoughts turned once again to the notion of the Camino as our mother, inspirer, and teacher. I decided that motherhood was a two-sided coin: one side the nurturer, the other the launcher.

Perhaps it was due to the female energy surrounding me for the last week and a half, but it seemed that there had been an abundance of caring, helping, inspiring, and teaching so far. This had come not only from Margarite, but from others as well, including me. I thought about this phase of my own journey in raising our sons. The nurturing part of motherhood came easily to me. Nurturing almost seemed effortless while still requiring enormous effort, if that makes any sense. Would it really be too trite to say that the nurturing aspect of motherhood had flowed out of me as easily as breast milk? The nurturing side of the coin was an essential ingredient for the early stages of life.

But the flip side of the coin was equally essential. The flip side involved separation, in equal measure for mother and child. It involved separation—not just in letting go, but of actively getting off of the path and out of the way so the child can move freely along his or her own path. It meant being a bystander, but a bystander like no other. With this side of the coin came freedom for both mother and child…freedom, exhilaration, but also at times terror at being alone on the path.

I thought of our boys. They, of course, were charting their own path long before I moved out of their way. It is a dilemma for mothers to get out of the way of their children, while still carrying the deep bond and attachment—and also the worry. I decided that I would use the Camino as a time to foster and enhance the letting-go side of me, sending them daily blessings and love.

As I walked along, still leaning hard against the wind, I did feel free from Margarite's guidance. In so many ways it was appreciated, but often it felt like it was raining down on me. Now I could walk as far and as fast as I chose or stop whenever I pleased. I was charting my own days, now, and it felt great. I was my own mother. The angst of being alone had not yet kicked in.

Toward the end of the walk through the *Meseta*, I had a fierce urge to pee. There were, of course, no cafés or bars anywhere. I spied a bridge just ahead and hoped that I might find a bit of privacy under the bridge. When I got there, I walked around the side of the bridge, and quickly, (quick enough to amaze myself!), got my pants down, squatted, and oh, the relief. Women have the greatest challenge of peeing outside, and I wondered if the winds might blow the pee back on my socks, pants and leg. Happily, it didn't. As I stood up, and was zipping up my pants, a German lady walked under the bridge and assessed what I had just done. Then she said the oddest thing: "Peeing ezz zee most natural zing, and besides, we all have zee white bottoms." Truly, how odd.

Finally out of the grain fields, I walked several kilometers until I found a café. In spite of being in a smoke-filled, cramped little room, it was wonderful to sit down and drink a hot cup of coffee. I met a young woman, a postdoctoral student, and we chatted awhile. Always the best part of my pilgrimage was the people I was meeting. She told me that she was researching a cure for HIV, and she had come here for a holiday. Holiday? I would have chosen a Caribbean island for my holiday!

That afternoon, I arrived at the small, dusty town of Hornillos. There was barely a town center, but I did find a store and bought some provisions for dinner—cheese, olives, tortellini, and pepperoni. The shopkeeper said the weather would be bad for the next three days. Great. I walked to the *albergue*, hoping it might be open. *Albergues* didn't usually open until three p.m., and it was only two p.m. It was not only open, but filled except for one bed, which thankfully I got. I wondered if the crowding related to the fact that this was a holy year on the Camino. Any year in which St. James's birthday, July 25, fell on a Sunday was considered a holy year. I had read that special significance was attached to walking during a holy year, thereby increasing the number of pilgrims. With that in mind, I had hoped that there would not be overcrowding so early in my walk;

but just after I had arrived, a huge group of pilgrims appeared. All had to be turned away.

This *albergue* was spare and small, with only one bathroom for twenty pilgrims. There were two rooms: a general area with a small kitchen, a long wooden table, and a fireplace; while the other room was filled with bunk beds. There was no heat, and the fire barely managed the job of heating the kitchen and dining area. The cold had turned us all grumpy, and again I had no interest in being friendly.

While Logroño had been filled with young bikers, this place was filled with old snorers! Everyone seemed to be napping, even at two p.m. I took the last available bed, a top bunk with no ladder. I painfully managed to hoist myself up and stretched out on the lumpy bed for a several-hour nap.

After my nap, I went into the main room and began preparing dinner.

A large and loud group of Germans had commandeered the only table and all of the chairs, while drinking and singing songs. I, along with the rest of the pilgrims, stood around the edges of the room. I managed to cook my pasta in a cup in the microwave, adding bits of cheese and pepperoni for flavor. I knew this was not enough dinner, but I was certainly not going out. Even sharing some of my olives with other pilgrims did not lighten my mood. I was certain that at some point the singing pilgrims would realize that the rest of us needed a chance to sit at the table, but they continued singing and drinking, oblivious to the rest of us. I was becoming crankier by the minute.

After my so-called dinner, I went back to the freezing bunk room, where I encountered an Italian couple. They seemed to be in some kind of distress. I asked if they were okay, and, with a bit of basic English and much sign language I learned that this was their first day, they were horrified by the *albergue*, and were genuinely surprised by the weather. I noticed that she was wearing a small knitted hat, and pointed to it, saying that she was so clever to know to bring a knitted hat to Spain in May! That helped only a little.

Finally, at 6:15 p.m., after brushing my teeth and taking some of the prescription antibiotic I had brought (still coughing; I didn't want whatever I had going on to turn into pneumonia), I washed my socks in the cold water. My hands were frozen, my nose was dripping, and this was my first night on the Camino without a shower. I again hoisted myself onto my top bunk. Fully dressed, I crawled into my sleeping bag with only my runny, freezing nose peeking out. What else was there to do but sleep? This was awful. I wanted to shoot myself. Why does anyone do this? Why was *I* doing this?

DAY 12

May 5, 2010

Hornillos del Camino to Castrojeriz

Most of the pilgrims left early and walked out into the freezing morning. Not me. It was still so cold inside the *albergue* that I stayed hunkered down in my sleeping bag until 7:15 a.m. I was the last pilgrim to leave the *albergue*.

The walking to Castrojeriz was easy, and the day would have been spectacular were it not for the cold. I stopped at a bar and enjoyed a cup of steaming tea along with (yet another) sandwich of thinly sliced, salty ham. I was beginning to tire of Spanish ham.

After walking for six hours, I finally arrived in Castrojeriz. I decided to stay in a small hotel and didn't feel the least bit of Camino guilt, as I had already decided to periodically treat myself to this indulgence. Especially after last night, I rationalized that I had earned it. The mental (and physical) payoff of a bit of comfort and quiet was worth it.

I checked into a small, nondescript hotel, and for only twenty-eight Euros enjoyed a private room with dinner and breakfast included. For only six additional Euros I could get clean laundry! I took a short nap and then decided to take a shower. It had been two days since my last. The shower was small—so small that I hardly fit. The shower curtain hung on a circular rod that extended beyond the actual shower floor, but the curtain barely reached the floor. How, I wondered, would the water stay inside the shower enclosure? I stepped in, turned on the water, and inched around in circles trying to wet my body. I continued turning (and trying to lather) like a pig on a barbecue spit. As I was turning, gulp, I lost my balance. I unfortunately grabbed for the shower curtain, and it, along with the shower rod and my wet, slippery body, crashed to the floor. The floor was now flooded with water. Momentarily stunned, I finally managed to stand up and turn off the water. Good God. Then, as best I could, I mopped the floor with the hotel's small, thin towels, and then dried myself with my own small, thin towel. How would I explain this to the Spanish-speaking innkeeper? I got dressed, gathered up my dirty laundry for the innkeeper, and went to the reception area to describe, as best I could, my debacle with the shower curtain. The innkeeper was moderately understanding…or so it seemed.

I decided that I would explore the town, try to send an email to Bill, and return for the hotel dinner, my first real dinner in three days.

It seemed there was a bit of flow to my life. I realized that I was actually taking my emotional pulse throughout the day, and right now I was getting a good reading in spite of the weather. I had a sense of rhythm about this thing, about being a pilgrim. Up early, pack up, walk all day and experience a flood of impressions and ideas throughout a day of walking. Then, at the end of the day, find a bed, unpack, and eat. Every single day, inching closer to Santiago.

But even though there was some flow, I could also sense that I was becoming more jaded and cynical, less euphoric. Today while walking, I met a young Korean woman who told me in the most ecstatic way that the Camino gave her so much energy as she prayed and prayed while she walked. *PULLEEZZ*, I thought. I knew she had read that somewhere. I decided that the Camino gave me a giant pain in the ass, and I'd like to have a talk with Mr. Camino, and perhaps send him to the time-out chair. I knew I was in a valley, but couldn't seem to pull myself out of it. I had come here to say good-bye, again, to my mother while she got on with her own Camino; to divest myself of worry; and, if lucky, to encounter some spiritual illumination. I had not come to strengthen my character or build up my confidence through harsh conditions. I was open to the spirit, but where was it? Were a broken shower rod, a flooded bathroom or a table commandeered by rude pilgrims somehow my only enduring transcendent experiences? After all this effort, would I have only a few measly insights? I did not want to extend myself to anyone. I knew this kind of thinking and self-pity was toxic, but at the moment I was unwilling to change it.

But the Camino never failed to surprise me.

I went alone to dinner that night, and that was just fine with me. The dinner was a pedestrian and tasteless affair: nondescript brown meat (I am not even certain what it was), soggy pasta salad, yogurt, and the worst wine I'd had so far. I hadn't imagined that in this Rioja region bad wine was even possible. There was only a sprinkling of other people eating there, and I was not even certain if they were pilgrims. But there was another woman eating alone just beside my table. She had a broad, pleasant face, with shoulder-length, honey-colored hair. She reminded me of the actress Louise Fletcher, the Academy Award winner who had starred in *One Flew over the Cuckoo's Nest* years ago. She and I began chatting across our tables about the hideous weather, the bad food, and the awful wine. She soon joined me at my table. Her name was Eleanor, and she was a German psychologist walking the second half of the Camino. She told me that she had been inspired to walk after reading the book by a German comedian who had described many hilarious events during his walk, as well as all the lessons he had learned. Sharing his funny encounters reminded us of ours as well. She told me some mishaps that had happened to her, while I told her about the night in Roncesvalles when I couldn't find my bed.

After our laughter died down, she told me that she was here for spiritual reasons, as well as for a change of routine. She told me of her experience the previous night when her day had ended in an *albergue* with two Hungarian girls and a Hungarian *hospitaleiro*. They had spent the evening arm-in-arm singing Hungarian folk songs that had reminded her of her own Hungarian parents. She teared up as she described the cold and awful day that had ended with such warmth and belonging, and decided that she was meant to be there. Two hours ago, I had not even met her, and yet our conversation had been swept clean of pretense.

As I write the chapter about this flat, dull day, lightened only by my conversation with Eleanor, I realize that my writing is flat and dull as well. The blandness of my descriptions is reflective of that day—walking from breakfast to lunch to dinner with only intervening sameness. Every day is not a party.

DAY 13

May 6, 2010

Castrojeriz to Boadilla del Camino

David was right out of Australian central casting: tall, broad-shouldered, tanned, uncombed dirty blond hair, and wearing, of course, the bush hat. *Very attractive*, I thought as we both sipped our coffee and munched toast at the bar just at the edge of town. Was I in need of some male energy? He told me that he was a global hiker and had trekked all over the world, even in Nepal. This was his sixth "hike" (as he said) on the Camino, and it was by far "the very best of all. The people are the best." I agreed.

We then talked about the day on the *Meseta*, the fierce winds, and the awful *albergue* (he'd been in the same one) in Hornillos. This experienced hiker, this big, brawny man, agreed that the weather and the accommodations were some of the worst he'd encountered. "I am not a wimp, then?" He declared me not a wimp, and I felt affirmed.

He further suggested that I stop in the *albergue* in Boadilla del Camino, as it had some of the nicest *hospitaleiros* on the Camino. Boadilla was five kilometers short of my plan for the day (to get to Fromista), but I was learning to pay attention to this sort of advice. I figured those five kilometers could be easily made up. David and I wished each other well and we took off, he very much faster than I.

I felt better today and enjoyed the relatively easy walking. Even though it was cold, the day lacked the terrible energy-sapping winds. I loved the birds, the bit of sun, the clarity of the vistas. The day was beautiful, and I made note of that.

When I arrived in the town of Boadilla, I saw a spare, gray, desolate place that looked like a bombed-out war village. But once I checked into Albergue En el Camino, I sensed what David had meant about this place. There were flowers outside and a reflecting pool with a sculpture of a pilgrim in the yard. After I checked in and found my bunk, I relaxed in the small living area. There was art on the red and white walls, actual furniture for sitting, and music playing throughout. Home…it felt like a home, and the family owners had clearly made an effort to create this oasis for tired pilgrims.

My only concern was that it was freezing in the barn where the bunks were. I walked to the main desk, and asked if it might be possible to get some heat. I returned to the barn, and shortly afterwards a young man walked in. He was probably around thirty-five years old, thin, with a long, dark braid of hair falling down his back. He called out for the pilgrim who had requested heat. When I stood up, he said, "Are you really that cold?" I'm not sure why I did this, but I put my hand up to his cheek as proof! He smiled, and said, "What you need is a hug!" and proceeded to pick me up and twirl me around. I giggled, then blushed, then noticed his laughing. Who was I? A teenager blushing at the attentions of a young man, or a seriously old lady who had just hiked a good bit of the day and smelled like a pig. I was aware that I had not been touched in two weeks, and I was also aware how good it felt even with this much younger stranger. I wanted my husband, and I wanted even more touching.

The young man was Francisco, and it was his grandfather who had started the *albergue* fifty years ago with the goal of treating pilgrims with love. The family continued the tradition, with his mother cooking as well as painting the framed art which decorated the walls. I asked him if he'd ever walked the Camino. "Heavens no! I do not need to walk the Camino. Some pilgrims walk it five or six times, and then brag about it, showing off their certificate of completion. They don't even know why they are doing it. It becomes like a drug for them, but they are still their same rude selves. You are supposed to learn on the Camino. It is supposed to make you think. But they don't think; they just brag." Clearly I had touched a nerve.

On the way to dinner, I stopped to enjoy the sculpture, the reflecting pool, the beauty of the place. A Catholic priest in white vestments and leather sandals was conducting a service on the lawn with a smattering of pilgrims. I wondered if the priest had been walking in his vestments.

The dining room had several long, wooden, harvest tables and more art by Francisco's mother. Most seats were already taken by the time I arrived so I sat in a vacant seat with an already formed group. My experience so far had told me to expect a friendly welcoming into this bunch. My experience, however, led me astray, as these French men and women chatted away, oblivious to my presence. Though I wondered if it might be perceived as rude, I decided to relocate, not really caring how it was perceived. I found one other vacant seat and joined Mary and Jacques from France, John and Margaret from Ireland, and a middle-aged man from Sweden who was biking the Camino. The hot soup, baked chicken (my first in two weeks), and bread seemed more tasty knowing that a loving mother's hand had fixed it just for us.

The conversation was constant and fun in spite of the language challenges. Exchanges were largely facilitated by ongoing charades. It was a lighthearted evening, not the sort with the heavier conversations from the first two weeks.

As I left to return to the barn, Francisco said, "I will miss you when you leave." While I seriously doubted that, this attention from a man filled some empty space I'd not even known was there. As I watched him he seemed to know just whatever medicine each pilgrim needed.

I got into my bunk ready for bed before many of the others. There were Spanish men who would not shut up, there were Italian men who got undressed in front of everyone, and I thought how indifferent I was at seeing this nudity. There were plenty of other pilgrims with their smelly bottoms on view. I went to sleep that night noting that I'd probably been exposed to way too much male flesh for one day.

DAY 14

May 7, 2010

Boadilla del Camino to Villalcazar de Sirga

I was halfway on my walk, but that meant that I still had halfway left. Ugh!

Today was going to be a big one, as I planned to walk all the way to Carrión de los Condes. After a breakfast of toast and coffee, and a hug from Francisco, I left, walking toward the town of Fromista, heading toward Carrión de los Condes. My brain was flooded with thoughts, mostly of the anxious variety. I found myself questioning everything. Could I really manage this for two and a half more weeks? Would I remain alone or try to connect with other pilgrims? Was it going to be like this for the rest of the pilgrimage? Had I made a big, fat stupid mistake? Who did I think I was?

The rhythm of the walking eventually moved me away from so many thoughts about myself.

Along the way, I met a lovely Frenchman who showed me photos of his family. He was clearly so proud. And so homesick. I told him how much I understood. Getting out of my own head always seemed to help. Later, in Fromista, I also met two Americans (bringing the number of Americans I'd met up to three). They were a mother and son from Montana. Steven, the son, was studying in Spain, and had decided to walk the Camino with his mother (who looked young enough to be his girlfriend, which I thought she was!). Janet, the mother, had joined him for his last two weeks of walking. In my sour mood, I asked Steven if he had told his mother how hard it was going to be. "I've tried to tell her," said this fit, young man, "but she just won't believe me." She prattled on and on about the wonder and fun and excitement of it all. *Just you wait.*

The early afternoon was sunny enough that I was even able to take off one of my jackets, something I'd not been able to do for days. There was hope.

No sooner than I had these thoughts, the skies opened up and pelted me with rain, soaking my boots, socks, and pants, and freezing my hands. WHY WAS I DOING THIS?

Shortly, the Irish couple from the previous night, John and Margaret, walked up behind me. They had decided, in part because of the horrible weather, to stop that day's walk in Villalcazar de Sirga (just five kilometers short of Carrión) and spend the night in the Monastery de Santa Clara. Not only would a private room there offer a respite from the *albergues*, but they also liked the name of the monastery as their daughter's name was Claire. Pilgrims made the oddest decisions for the oddest reasons. I decided to join them, as the idea of a warm, private room with my own bathroom percolated in my mind.

Once we arrived, I checked in with the *hospitaleiro*, Eduardo, a nervous and unhelpful man. He gave me three ancient keys that opened three different entrances to what would be my room. The outer doors were unusually thick and were carved in ornate detail. If I had not been so wet and frozen, I might have appreciated their beauty. When I finally got into my room, I instantly noticed the bathtub and began imagining the long, luxurious soak I would soon be enjoying. But I also noticed that there was no heat in the room.

I went back out to the reception area to ask Eduardo if the heat issue could be remedied. This was my second night of requesting heat. What was going on?

Returning to my room, I now became aware that I didn't know which thick, carved door was the actual one which led to my room. I tried the keys, which were hard to manage, until one finally opened the door I needed. I took a short nap under a blanket while waiting for the heat to come on.

When I woke up, there was a clanking noise coming from the radiator and I felt encouraged that things would be toasty in short order. I went into the bathroom happily anticipating my soak. There was a tub, there was a shower curtain, now there was heat, and there was hot water. There was hot water! Yes! But wait. There was no plug for the bathtub drain! Damn! My quick, un-soaky shower was simply not the same thing.

I washed my clothes, hoping the heat now gradually coming into the room would dry them by the next morning. I tried unsuccessfully to call Bill, and tried, though not very hard, to focus on something positive. I was dry, clean, warm, and halfway through my pilgrimage.

I left the monastery to find a café for dinner. My first stop was a smoky, dirty bar, its floor covered with cigarette butts, its only clients old men playing cards. Nope. This wouldn't do.

The next café seemed better and it advertised a cheap (ten Euros) pilgrim meal. But there were no single seats. The hostess had one table with four chairs, and pointed me toward it. I was warm, dry, and would soon be full. Things were looking up.

Shortly, three white-haired gentlemen walked into the café, and saw that all the tables were taken. I motioned for them to join me, and they made their way over through the crowded room. It occurred to me that these were the same Frenchmen who last night snubbed me in Boadilla. An interesting turn of events. I learned, through the translations of one of them, that they were retired businessmen who walked two weeks on the Camino each year, and who, after those two weeks of walking, were joined by their wives for some high Camino living. They didn't seem to fit the mold of other pilgrims I had met so far. Why were they doing this? Exercise? Sport? Adventure? Vacation?

We enjoyed our pilgrim dinner while talking nonstop. We managed to talk about Obama's health care plan, Sarkosy, their occupations, nudity in the *albergues* (with my doing a bit of charades), their children, and finally, and for the longest time, the differences between northern and southern Europeans. They sneered with disgust as they described the southern Europeans, whom they referred to as "Mediterraneans," and boasted about the superior qualities of northern Europeans. I was taken aback by their blatant prejudice and tried to engage them in a discussion of tolerance, citing as many examples as I could from the United States. Their response, simply and succinctly, was to ask me why there was still so much racial discord in America. My unfair attempt to put them in their place resulted in my being put into mine. A change of subject kept the dinner from being one of divided opinions on race and status. We are all guilty.

DAY 15

May 8, 2010

Villalcazar de Sirga to Terradillos de los Templarios

At breakfast, Janet, the American mother walking with her student son, was explaining, "It is impossible to hold both fear and gratitude in the brain at the same time. It can only be one or the other. They now know this through brain imaging, and we are also learning just how much plasticity there is in the brain. We are discovering that by focusing on gratitude we can create and shape neural pathways and we are beginning to believe this can help with the treatment of fear and anxiety. Exciting stuff!" This had been part of Janet's dissertation research. And this was BEFORE coffee! This was the aspect of the Camino that I totally adored! I filed away what she was saying, said my good-byes, and headed out for the long thirty-kilometer day, hoping I'd run into her son and her again.

I was walking to Terradillos de los Templarios and pushing myself, trying to stick to my schedule. This would be the last time I'd attempt such a distance, but for the moment I was ready to go.

While the way was flat, it was another cold and rainy day, with few places to stop, adding to the challenges. I was not at all mindful about hydrating, as my attention was focused on trying to stay warm.

Finally, after about twenty kilometers, I found a café, and stopped for lunch and a rest. The place was smoky, the floor strewn with cigarette butts, and there were piles of the damp packs and boots of other pilgrims. I could practically see the steam rising from so much wet hiking gear. My ham and cheese sandwich (more ham—ugh) arrived on greasy, half-toasted bread, but I devoured it, as I was starving. Before leaving, I used the bathroom. It was filthy, with a clogged toilet, but better than my several adventures of peeing in the open fields on the way here. What was I manifesting?

The last ten kilometers were along the asphalt shoulder of the highway, walking which was always more challenging for the knees, ankles, and feet. As the day wore on, I knew I was wearing out, yet I saw no waymarkers indicating how much farther I had to go. According to my map, I knew I was walking in the right direction. The path was totally straight, and I'd made no turns. I sensed a rising fear when I suddenly remembered my conversation with Janet this morning: "Our brains cannot hold fear and gratitude at the same time." I decided to focus on gratitude in this moment and see if it helped at all. *I am grateful that my legs have no cramps. I am grateful that my feet are dry.* I continued this practice all the way up my body until I got to my head, *I am grateful not to have a headache.* As ridiculous as I felt, I had to admit that I was less grumpy and anxious. At least the fear, which I knew wouldn't help, seemed to have receded, and the little gratitude practice had provided a bit of distraction. Prone as I was to anxiety, I would have to remember this back in my real life.

After my gratitude exercise, I decided to pray—first to Mom, then Dad, then, finally, to God. *Help me to get to this* albergue. *I am so weary. If I'm lost, please help me notice the waymarkers to get me moving in the right direction. Please, help.* I didn't know what else to do.

Within minutes, a young woman rode up on her bike. I flagged her down, and asked if she knew where the Los Templarios *albergue* was. We compared her map to my guidebook, and both determined that it had to be close. But where was it? She suggested that she ride to the top of the small hill, and if she saw it, she would wave me on. If she didn't see it, she would ride back and we'd figure out a new plan. As she rode off, I thought about how quickly help seemed to arrive on the Camino. Think it, and it comes. This happened over and over, here. Did it happen like this back home, and I had just failed to notice it? Or was the help not always in the exact form I'd imagined?

Shortly I saw her waving me toward the top of the hill, shouting, "Just beyond the hill!" Then she rode off. She had been like an angel who had appeared at the exact moment. It was kind of amazing.

Very soon I was happily checking into this new, modern, and clean *albergue*. I was certain that a warm shower and a good meal would restore me.

However, as I started the checking-in process with the helpful *hospitaleiro*, Tanya, I began feeling sick to my stomach. I asked Tanya to guide me to the bathroom, which she promptly did. Once inside the bathroom, I barely made it to the toilet before I had a violent bout of vomiting and diarrhea. It occurred so quickly that I hardly had time to process what was happening. Maybe I was sick from the disgusting sandwich I'd eaten earlier. I figured I would start to feel better, and headed back to the check-in counter.

As I continued the check-in process, I almost immediately felt weaker and I knew that I would be sick again. I told Tanya that I needed to sit down, and she took me to a chair just at the entrance. That was the last thing I remembered. I passed out.

When I regained consciousness, an army of angels was ministering to me. Tanya was patting my hands and speaking frantically to me in Spanish; Carlos, the short, round-faced Spaniard with the broad smile, was lightly smacking my face; and, finally, Eleanor, from several nights ago, was informing me that the rescue squad was on its way. I had the brief thought that I might be dying.

The medics arrived, moving slowly and calmly, and showing no alarm. That was a good sign. They performed the routine diagnostic tests: blood pressure (90/60), pulse, etc.; scribbled notes on a pad of paper, and declared me "dehydrated and depleted. She needs to rest, drink plenty of water, and a salty, Gatoraid-type drink." As slowly as they had arrived, they left. Eleanor gently admonished me for not drinking enough water throughout the day. She further added that getting sick and dehydrated was no big deal, and that this sort of thing happened routinely to pilgrims. Easy for her to say "no big deal"; it felt like a really big deal to me! We were able to get Bill on the phone to let him know what had transpired. He spoke with all of my helpers, and we even managed some laughter as I reassured him that I was beginning to feel fine.

In truth, I didn't feel fine. I felt horrible, weak, still sick, and so vulnerable.

Tanya led me to a small room with two sets of bunk beds and a private bathroom. I was not so out of it that I didn't appreciate these welcome accommodations. The room was empty of other pilgrims, though I was too spent to even care. The bathroom came in handy as I continued to vomit and experience diarrhea throughout the evening.

Eventually, I settled on one of the bottom bunks, and drifted in and out of sleep. About every thirty minutes either Carlos or Eleanor came in to check on me. At one point, Carlos brought me an extra blanket, as I was freezing. I wasn't sure if there was a problem with heat in the room or if I was just experiencing chills. Carlos said, "I Poppa." Yes, but I want my Momma!

Later, a middle-aged woman came to the room furious that I apparently was in "her" bed. She screamed at me as I tried to explain my situation. She was not satisfied, but her yelping brought Tanya who escorted the angry woman to another room. The room was later filled with three warm, compassionate people who could not have been more solicitous.

At seven thirty p.m., feeling a bit better, I brushed my teeth and took a shower. Cleanliness helped, but only a bit. I went to the dining room to see if I could tolerate any food. When I walked in, a cheer went up. Seriously? Just for managing to stand upright and walk into the dining room? It did add to my sense of being cared for. Carlos encouraged me to continue to drink the salty concoction that was meant to restore me. Even though I knew it was what I needed, I could hardly manage to get it down, much less the omelette that he was also insisting I eat. Eleanor was there, cheering me on to health. She told me that her foray on the Camino was over, and she was heading back to Germany, as she could no longer tolerate the weather.

After a brief time in the dining room, I went back to my room, having decided to go to sleep. I had no thoughts about my schedule, or what might come next. I felt utterly unmoored as my carefully constructed plan seemed to be slipping away. The only thoughts I had were about compassion, so much of which had come my way this evening. Maybe the Big Spirit I had been seeking was being evidenced by the many acts of my fellow pilgrims and the kind *hospitaleiros*.

DAY 16

May 9, 2010

Terradillos de los Templarios to León

My focus and enthusiasm had disappeared along with much of what had been in my body. When I awoke, there was no heat in the room or hot water. After dressing, I joined Eleanor for the tiniest bit of breakfast as we both commiserated about the weeklong forecast for bad weather. Why were we doing this, and what were we supposed to be learning? After she left, I sat limply in the waiting area of the *albergue* and overheard an Italian couple making arrangements for a taxi to León. Without regret at not walking, nor embarrassment at intruding on their plan, I asked if there might be room for one more. They said they would be delighted for me to join them.

When the taxi arrived, we tossed our packs into the trunk, got in, and were off on the sixty-kilometer ride to León. I had no plan, and oddly didn't even care. This was not how I did things. I always had a plan, for everything. I had planned well in advance for trips we had taken. I planned our finances a year in advance, and was proud that at any given moment I could let Bill know where we had extra money for whatever purchase we'd contemplated. I had planned how to spend my retirement years, and if I had not been routinely discouraged from doing so, I would have planned the lives of our sons. I loved planning. I was good at it. I understood the control aspect of planning, but I didn't care. In fact, I thought control had gotten an unfairly bad rap. Control helped me stay organized, and let others know they could depend on me. Control had helped me care for my family, go to graduate school while working full time, and a million other things while making it look simple. Planning and control were my old friends, but ones who provided me often with frustration when the plan didn't stay as I'd envisioned it. As I rode along in the taxi, I thought that I was plan-free today, out of control. I had no idea what was going to happen next, where I'd sleep tonight, how I'd get back to being a pilgrim. I was simply too weak to fight it. I gave in. This was new territory for me, and I recognized a big, fat Camino lesson smacking me in the face.

Mid-morning, the taxi dropped me off at the Albergue Santa Maria de Carbajal in León, while the Italians continued on. This large and well-run *albergue* was managed by the Benedictine nuns. I dragged my pack up the steps and knocked on the door. Nothing. I knocked again, longer and more loudly, until finally, Juan, the Spanish *hospitaleiro*, arrived to tell me that it was too early to admit pilgrims. "I've been sick. Would it be possible to just sit inside?" He opened the large door and let me in.

He said that since I was recuperating, I could stay in the small, private room next to the men's dormitory—though I might be required to share it. When I got to the room, I was pleased to see that it also had a private bathroom. I was still making frequent trips to the bathroom.

I took a nap of several hours and decided to shower when I awoke. Once again, as had happened in Castrojeriz, water squirted all over the floor as I tried to shower. I mopped up the mess as best I could. When I was finally dressed, I sat on the bed crying like a baby, so tired of dealing with things on the Camino.

After a bit of dinner out in León, which helped only marginally, I returned to the room for an earlier than usual bedtime. As I lay in the bed thinking about the day and the unfolding events, I wasn't sure what the next days would hold, or how far away I was from Santiago, or how long I'd feel so rotten. The only thing that I really knew for certain was that I could not imagine picking up my pack and walking. I had been reduced to sleeping and the simplest of bodily functions.

DAY 17

May 10, 2010

León

I thought that by mid-morning I would be feeling better, but I thought wrong. I ached everywhere… my arms, my legs, head, stomach, and back. I was entirely depleted of energy, and even wondered if I might need to be in a hospital. I could not think of manifestations or spiritual experiences. All I wanted to do was die.

As I lay in the bed feeling sorry for myself, an idea began to form in my mind. It formed ever so slightly at first, but the more I considered it, the stronger it got. At first I couldn't even contemplate what I was thinking, but the more I thought, the more it took on momentum until it was a fully formed plan rooted in my mind. Of course it made perfect sense! Why hadn't I considered it before? It was so obvious! I was going home! The list of reasons lined up in my head like little soldiers at a review. It was not as if I hadn't been walking the Camino; I'd walked for two and a half weeks—so what if I didn't get all the way to Santiago? I could always come back. So what if I didn't get my *Compostela*? I didn't need some certificate to verify my efforts, and besides that I was old—maybe too old to have ever taken off in the first place. It had been a bad idea from the start. Who did I think I was? Big Spirit? Give me a break! Soon I would be home with Bill whom I had left for five weeks. What an incredibly stupid thing to do. In no time I would be in my own house, in my own bed, soaking in my own tub. I would be eating American food, seeing my friends, seeing my boys, one of whom was now engaged. Yes, I had a wedding to think about. I was happy and feeling energized. I had a plan. I would call Bill, and I knew he would understand.

Even though my early phone call woke him up, Bill did understand. He just didn't think it was a very well-considered idea. Shouldn't I think about it a little longer and consider the consequences? He speculated that in the long run I might really feel disappointed. Shouldn't I try to hold on a bit longer? Also, he wondered about the extra expense of changing my flight plan, to say nothing of his plan to spend a week in Spain, after being alone for such a long time. It was only in retrospect that I became aware of how totally blinded I was by my own interests, with so little consideration for his. In the end, he agreed to check into flight changes, and told me to sit tight until we talked again.

Sit tight? I was practically dancing with delight. No more *albergues*. No more Spanish ham, or wind, or rain, or being a stranger. I was going home!

I quickly dressed and headed for the reception area. I needed to find Juan because I knew his knowledge of English would help me in getting a ticket back to Madrid, and then back to Alexandria. When I got to the desk, there was no Juan, only two elderly Spanish gentlemen who spoke no English. "Can you please tell me where Juan is?" Blank stare. "I need to speak to Juan." I spoke more loudly this time just in case they hadn't understood my previous request. "I have to get a ticket to Madrid." I was now practically screaming and that brought in the old nun dressed in her black habit. I turned to her and continued, "I need to find Juan who can help me get a ticket—airoplano (flapping my arms). I need to go home—*casa, casa*—to my husband (pointing to my wedding band). I've been sick. I've got to get home. I can't do this anymore." And then, do not ask me why, I threw my arms around the nun and began sobbing and sputtering, "Help me. Please help me. I've got to get home."

Almost as I uttered those words, I became aware of other people in the waiting area. I glanced up, still clinging to the nun, tears sliding down my face, and found I was staring at the most handsome young man...tan, mops of blond hair, and a broad smile.

"What's wrong? I speak English. I can help."

"I've got to get home. Can you help me get a ticket to Madrid? I've been sick. I made a mistake. I've just got to get home."

He and the old nun began talking back and forth, and he was translating for both of us.

"The nun says you need to calm down."

"Calm down! I need to get home!"

"She says this sort of thing always happens to pilgrims. It's just not that big a deal. You need to rest, and you can do that right here for several days. You'll be fine."

I would not be fine. I was starting to panic. Maybe they were not hearing me, or understanding me, or really getting the level of my distress. It sounded like they were trying to talk me out of my plan.

He told me that his name was Franz, that he was from Germany, and then he suggested that we go into the kitchen. "We are all sick," he said, pointing to the young man and woman with him. "This is David from England, and Maria from Poland, both of whom have tendonitis. I've got it as well. We are all going to rest here until we can walk again."

Maria fixed us all some broth, which tasted heavenly. Maybe I could cope for a few hours. Franz suggested that I go back to bed and told me he'd check on me throughout the day. But I wanted to go home.

I went back to my room and rested for most of the day. Just as he'd promised, Franz checked on me periodically. He brought me soup, and then sweetened chamomile tea, and finally a bouquet of flowers. It was then that I remembered that yesterday was Mother's Day. Toward the end of the day, he returned just to talk. I asked him to tell me his story, which he eagerly did. He had come on the Camino because he was so depressed about his life but he could not imagine getting any more therapy. He and his brother had thought this might be a good activity for him. He told me about his two sons, his Harvard education, and the fact that I reminded him of his mother who had also walked the Camino. He was the first person I'd met who was walking the Camino because of depression. He also told me that one of the priests had praised him today in front of a group of schoolchildren because he had been the epitome of a "good pilgrim" due to his kindness to me. The priest had told the children that he had arrived just in time to take care of the sick and tired lady. (I was certain the priest had been wondering how to shut up the old wacko American.) The more he talked, the more manic he seemed as he described the Camino as "the very best thing in the world." As he continued to talk, his elevated mood became more somber, and he choked up and began to cry. As he cried, so did I. We were a Camino mess.

He told me that he had a very strong feeling that I needed to finish my pilgrimage, however I did it, whether walking or by bus. "This will be a gift to your friends, and besides, miracles can happen along the way." I thought that maybe I had conjured him for just this message, but NO! NO! NO! I didn't care about the Camino anymore. I didn't want to hear what he was saying. I never wanted to pick up my pack again, or walk in the rain, or sit in a smoky bar, or sleep in an *albergue*. I argued with him that part of knowing yourself was knowing when to STOP something, as well as when to push through a difficulty. "No."

He wasn't buying it. "Stop to get better, to rest, but don't stop altogether." Then he finally said something that seemed to make a bit of sense. "If you are sick, the last thing you want to be doing is traveling, queuing up, going through security, finding a taxi or hotel in Madrid—in short, negotiating international travel."

By the end of the day, I had decided to continue and finish my pilgrimage. I am not totally certain how I traveled from the certainty that I was going home to the certainty that I wasn't. I just knew that I did get there. It was not that Franz convinced me with his logic or encouragement, but rather through his care and attention he enabled the decision that was always there, deep in the recesses of my mind, to be revealed. I simply hadn't wanted or been able to acknowledge it.

I called Bill—poor Bill, who had been yanked all over the emotional landscape today—and told him that I would not be coming home, that there would be no need to alter the travel arrangements, that he was not to worry. I was so sorry. I told him that somehow I would finish my pilgrimage, though I did not know how.

DAY 18

May 11, 2010

León

The serenading from the men's dorm, right next door, woke me up. Burping, farting, snoring, singing, laughing. Good Lord! I felt somewhat better, which was a welcome relief, and something I'd not felt for days. I glanced at my watch: 6:30 a.m. I got up, and brushed my teeth just in case Franz decided to pop in and say good-bye. I had no sooner thought that than I heard a slight knock on the door. Sure enough, when I opened the door, Franz stood there, smiling, dressed, and ready for a day of hiking.

"Who will take care of you today?"

"Believe it or not, I am feeling a little better. That's a good sign, right? In fact, I'm going to try to take care of David [the young Englishman who was recovering from tendonitis] and pay it forward just a bit. I bet I look like crap with my gray hair sticking straight up."

"It doesn't matter. We are *peregrinos*."

We hugged, I wished him well, thanked him for his many kindnesses, and said, "Take care, dear friend."

He was off in the pouring rain, and I went back to bed.

I finally got up around mid-morning, and checked on David. He told me that he had walked from France, and was walking all the way to Portugal to try and figure out his young life. He told me that he would be eating nothing today while his body was about the business of healing itself. "Bodies are designed to heal if we just get out of their way." Had I been in the way of my body's efforts to heal itself? He did agree to a cup of tea, which I fixed for him. This simple effort for someone else seemed to have an immediate effect on me—a positive effect.

I left the *albergue* to get a croissant, as the slightest hunger rumblings had started. Even though few places were open, I was able to get my croissant. However, on the way back to the *albergue*, I became lost. When I finally found the *albergue*, it was locked. Everything was such a damned ordeal. Finally, the cleaning lady let me in, and I went right to my little room for more sleep, exhausted by this simple excursion.

When I next woke up, it was late afternoon. I could tell that the sun was trying to peek through the clouds. I had a long telephone conversation with Bill, trying to undo all the earlier drama, and to assure him that all was well. I'd finish my walk. I told him again I was feeling better. Not exactly lying, but not exactly telling the truth.

When the sun was fully out, I headed out into the city of León to find an internet café, and possibly some dinner. I bought a few items for

David, sent massive emails to my family, ran into the three French businessmen from several nights ago, and, in short, behaved more like a pilgrim and less like an invalid.

I found a café close to the *albergue* and decided to have my first real meal in days. Happily it was open even at the early hour of five p.m., it was smoke free, and the owners were incredibly caring and attentive in bringing me a meal that would work for me. My dinner of plain baked chicken, rice with vegetables, and a pot of hot tea was exactly what I needed. I could feel myself getting stronger with each bite.

When I returned to the *albergue*, I gave David the small gifts: a notebook and pen and lemon drops, for which he was appropriately grateful. I then helped several new pilgrims with how things worked here. I felt like part of the staff, and realized I was actually feeling a little sad to be leaving.

But thinking of leaving quickly brought me to the realization that I had no clue what was next in store. I still couldn't imagine how I'd pick up my pack in the morning and start walking again. I wasn't sure what the weather predictions were nor was I sure how far I would be able to get. I wasn't sure of anything.

As I prepared for bed, my mind was flooded with musings from the past several days:

- I had once read that when we encounter a paradox, we have encountered truth. You die in order to be reborn; or, my dad's favorite: "I love you, but I don't always love your behavior." So I am my behavior, but I am not only my behavior? Paradox = truth. On the Camino I kept hearing that it was the journey toward the cathedral, not the actual arrival, that was the significant part of the pilgrimage. But can there be a journey without a destination? Getting to Santiago seemed to be driving us all.

– When Bill had told his brother, an Episcopalian priest, about my troubles, he said, "Pilgrimages are hard for a reason. They are about mortification of the flesh, followed by release, and then salvation." What? Why was I just now hearing this?

– In my email to Bill today, I said that, "There is life after death, maybe just a little." Low, low points were often followed by new understandings, insights, and fresh energy— if we noticed. Resurrection was such a helpful concept because as a species we are so hopelessly flawed. Resurrection paved the way for forgiveness, self-forgiveness, and starting over.

– Thoughts of flawed humans made me think of my old nemesis, my desire for and pursuit of perfection. I was first aware of my need for perfection in Miss Martin's second-grade class. Miss Martin was a perfect teacher: pretty, patient, soft-spoken, and kind; so kind that when I spilled the fishbowl one afternoon and I'd stayed back to help her clean the classroom, she did not get the least bit angry. With the shattered glass, spreading water, and flopping goldfish, she said that people made mistakes and that it was okay. I had not thought it was okay. I didn't want to make mistakes with Miss Martin. I didn't want them anywhere.

During morning writing practice, any mistake on my paper would send me to her desk asking for another piece of paper so I could start over and write the lesson perfectly. Usually by my seventh request she would say, "No, Robin. No more paper. Go back and fix what you have or turn it in like it is. It is okay to make mistakes. Everybody does." Stinging tears filled my eyes as I returned to my seat with my imperfect paper.

Eventually my pursuit of perfection proved exhausting, and always perfection was just out of reach. I eventually learned to try my best at things, and to try, though it was hard, to be satisfied with less than perfect results. However, with brand-new activities, like motherhood, or graduate school, or my first job, my old friend would resurface until I had, once again, put it in its proper and more appropriate place.

It therefore shouldn't have been surprising that as I started this 500-mile walk I did so with an earnest attempt at being a perfect pilgrim. Just as I had tried to throw away my imperfect second-grade writing, I had also tried to discard my flawed and messy pilgrimage, an adventure filled with vomiting, fainting, and, of all things, Spanish public transportation! It occurred to me that maybe my pilgrimage was not ruined but now simply one filled with incredible high points and painful low ones. Maybe it was exactly the one I needed, the one I'd manifested to teach me one more time about the perils of perfection.

As I prepared for bed and packed up, I thought about the first part of the pilgrimage, which had been filled with such connections to others; I thought about this middle part, where I mostly found myself alone and disconnected from others; and finally, I was imagining the last part, hoping for health and strength, hoping for better weather, hoping to be reconnecting again to other pilgrims. I also decided that I would try to avail myself of the landscape, the churches, and the sights I'd been uninterested in previously. I would stay in some hotels and I would definitely not get dehydrated again. I could do this. I *would* do this.

DAY 19

May 12, 2010

León to Astorga

My eyes pinged open. That was a good sign that my life force was returning. Time for Big Girl Panties!

Over coffee and crackers I talked with Juan, the wonderful *hospitaleiro* from my first day here in León. He had been a pilgrim and urged me to finish my walk—but "finish happy." Duly noted. I met Greta, the middle-aged Swedish nurse, also having coffee. She was going to Astorga today, but going by train while she recuperated from a pilgrim ailment. I looked out of the kitchen window, and it was raining—except not just raining. It was pouring buckets of rain, a torrential downpour. It was the kind of rain that if I'd been driving I'd have pulled over to the side of the road, as the wipers would have been unable to keep up. With that, I knew I'd be leaving today, but just not walking. I asked Greta if I might join her for the train ride to Astorga. That was fine with her, as she'd be glad to have the company. More help, and it was only eight thirty in the morning. I was a Camino slut—first the bus, then the taxi, and now a train!

"You can do this! You can do this! The worst is probably over. It will be okay." All morning, as I packed up I cheered myself on like a kid going to sleepover camp for the first time.

With laced boots, hoisted packs, and sticks in hand, Greta and I ran through the rain and jumped into a taxi that took us to the railway station for our four-hour wait for the train to Astorga. The station was packed with tons of travelers and other pilgrims. Some pilgrims were waiting with their sopping bikes that would have been impossible to ride in this rain.

That night, I wrote the following email to Bill:

> "It always amazes me that there are folks here with whom there is an instant connection, and tons of others who seem like bodies in the background. I have an instant connection with Greta. She is sixty-five, an intensive care nurse in Sweden by day, but an art historian in her soul. After grocery shopping and settling into the *albergue*, she and I went to the Astorga cathedral and its little museum. I loved seeing the writings from the 1100s. She sees so many things that never cross my mind. She points out one painting of a crucifixion where there is a gash in Jesus' stomach, and a figure in the painting has his hand in the gash trying to revive Jesus. She is intrigued by this from a medical

perspective, and takes a photo and emails it to her surgeon friends back in Sweden.

Back at the *albergue* I notice tons of little spirit. This place is beautiful, an ancient building, a fire burning in the fireplace, a large open area and kitchen with people cooking and talking, or relaxing or getting a massage on the two tables set up in the living room! Greta and I fix pasta, olives, apricots, and manchego cheese, my first real food in days. While we are eating and chatting and sipping our red wine (my first in a week), Doris joins us. She is a sixty-year-old earth mother from Holland who has longed to walk the Camino for thirty years and yet she is now very homesick for her husband, her children, and her little grandson named Robin. She is excited to show me her Robin tattoo just above her left breast. When she showed it to me, I couldn't imagine the pain involved in getting that tattoo, nor could I imagine her plan with subsequent grandchildren.

Then who shows up but Steven and Janet, the son and mother from Montana. They are with four Spanish judges whom they have befriended and with whom they have walked 30 kilometers each day in the rain for the past week. We have hugs all around, as we are delighted to run into each other again, and we hatch a plan to meet for breakfast the following day. I am once more carried away by these amazing people (who are also cranky about the weather). I cannot imagine another place where complete strangers come together like this. It's supposed to rain for two more days, but I'm back in love with the Camino. I miss you, and I love you. Robin"

PART THREE

DAY 20

May 13, 2010

Astorga to Rabanal del Camino

At long last the BIG SPIRIT came!! Just not to me…

The day had begun typically as we walked out of Astorga, but not so typically, as it was my first day of walking in four days. Greta stayed back, as she had more recuperating ahead of her. Doris, the Dutch earth mother—whom I quickly outpaced on this flat terrain—and I were heading to Rabanal. There was a merriment to the day as I bounced along—as if the intervening week had not even occurred. I loved walking on this sunny day, and was so grateful that I had not gone home.

I met handsome James, a recent law school graduate from Brazil, who, with his father and his father's friend, was starting his first day of walking for two weeks on the Camino before he was launched into adulthood. Their first-day honeymoon was easy to spot: enthusiasm, high energy, wonder and awe. James told me that they were writing a book about the Camino, a coffee-table book with photographs of scenery and pilgrims, along with all the varied pilgrim stories.

"Why are you walking?" he asked me.

"Spiritual reasons."

Then they peppered me with questions: "What were the *albergues* like? What had been hard? Were the people nice? What about the landscape? Food? Blisters?" They hung on my words as if I were the expert. Me—the expert!

I stopped at a café for food, water, and rest, mindful of taking it easy on this first day back on the walk. While munching on an apple, to my amazement Franz walked in, and we both screamed and hugged as if we'd known each other for our entire lives. Maybe we had gotten to know each other as well as people who *have* known each other always. He was thrilled that I was walking, and I was thrilled that he seemed less depressed.

I later walked part of the way with a Dutchman whom I'd met at the *albergue* back in Astorga. Denis was a charming, witty, middle-aged man who had already walked the Camino before, and, in fact, fished in the streams and rivers along the Camino. That was a first for me. He was going to Rabanal, where he was volunteering as a *hospitaleiro* for two weeks. Then he said, "If you ever can't find a place to stay, I'll save you a place in my bed because of your natural sex appeal." Good Lord. What was I giving off? And why suddenly did there seem to be men everywhere?

In the late afternoon, I arrived in Rabanal and checked in to the British-run Albergue Gaucelmo. The *hospitaleiros* there were American, and I had a brief flutter of homesickness for my own tribe when I talked to them. Even though the walking had been easy, and I'd taken great care to stop along the way to rest, drink water, and eat, I was exhausted. After unpacking, doing laundry, and showering, I sat in front of the small fireplace in the central living room and dozed off and on. Outstretched in front of the fireplace a man was receiving a massage. The man giving the massage was dressed only in black balloon pants, with a muscular, bare chest, and thick, long dreadlocks trailing down his back. There was a decidedly exotic air to his appearance. Eventually one of the *hospitaleiros* asked him to move along so that the other pilgrims could enjoy the fire.

The crackling warmth of the fire almost put me to sleep while Denis sat next to me chatting away. Eventually my stomach was rumbling with hunger, and I announced that I was going to dinner, even at this early our, so that I could then attend the Gregorian chants at the nearby medieval church later that evening.

Denis asked if he could join me for dinner, and while I felt done for the day, I acquiesced.

We walked across the street to the tiny restaurant and found a table near Harold and Gudrun, a Dutch man and a German woman. We struck up a conversation and learned that she was experiencing a version of "pilgrim flu" that featured an upset stomach. In spite of her sickness, we also learned that even though Harold was married, they had struck up a romance on the Camino. Their chemistry was palpable as they described meeting in the airport and recognizing their immediate and strong attraction. I had heard of Camino romances, but this was my first encounter.

After dinner, I excused myself and went to the church to hear the Gregorian chants only to discover that I had just missed them.

On my way out of the restaurant, I saw that Denis had joined the men from Brazil, as well as two young and beautiful Italian women. They had invited me to join them after the recital at the church. Even though I was weary from the day's walk, the energy of this group pulled me in. When I returned to the *albergue*, James was interviewing everyone at the table for his book. Maria, one of the Italian women, tall, slender, with dyed reddish hair, told us that she was on the Camino because of death. With tears in her eyes she told the story of her mother's recent death, but also, sadly, the death of her younger sister during a hiking accident. I had read that death was often a motivation for walking the Camino. I was certainly walking after the death of my mother, but this was the first other person that I had met who was walking because of death. I imagined the deep well of grief in this young woman.

Then James held the recorder in Denis's direction. Having spent some time with Denis today, and having become familiar with his wry sense of humor, I was expecting a lighthearted, funny story explaining his walk. I was totally wrong. He told us that he had walked the Camino because he'd been interested in hiking, exercise, nature, even fishing. Also, he had loved meeting the many amazing people on the Camino. What he was not at all interested in was religion or spirituality. He engaged us all with his descriptions of that first walk, but it was his description of the mass at the cathedral that really had us leaning in in order not to miss any of what he was saying. He had arrived at the cathedral, and had only decided to attend the daily mass because it had been recommended by his guidebook. He told us that he was standing quietly during the service, hardly paying attention, his mind wandering about his next big hike, when slowly at first, but then more strongly he was aware of a bolt of energy moving through his body. His voice was slow and measured, carefully saying each word perhaps to relive the experience or to make certain that we were understanding the gravity of what he was saying. He continued trying to explain something that he felt was inexplicable, and as he continued to talk, I felt a slight shiver moving through my body. Questions started pouring out of me: "What did you think? How had it made you feel?" He said that he had no adequate vocabulary to describe what had happened, but this experience had upended his life. He wondered if he was experiencing God entering his body. He said that he didn't believe in God, or at least that he hadn't believed in God. Now he wasn't sure. The only way that he had been able to make any sense of it was to come back and volunteer as a *hospitaleiro*. He was giving back by paying it forward.

When Denis finished talking, James turned off his tape recorder, and we all sat for several minutes, stunned and silent. Words were inadequate so we all hugged, and hugged for a really long time. We were all silent as we walked back to the *albergue*. BIG SPIRIT really had come.

DAY 21

May 14, 2012

Rabanal del Camino to Molinaseca

As Denis poured the coffee at breakfast, I apologized to those at my table for last night.

"I hope my outburst did not disturb you."

"Quite the contrary, we were grateful."

If you were grateful, I thought, *why had no one said anything?* The previous day had ended at 10:15 p.m. with the Spanish mother and her adult daughter laughing hysterically on their beds. It was hard to ascertain what was so funny as they broke the cardinal Camino rule of etiquette by disturbing others after 9:00 p.m. I had never heard such laughter. Well, I had heard it, usually in our family room with friends, a roaring fire, and a bottle of wine. I had just not heard it on the Camino, and certainly not at that hour.

I developed a slow, burning rage, and tried to figure out what to do, hoping another tired pilgrim would ask them to stop. My attempts at non-verbal communication—heavy sighing, tossing from side to side, clearing my throat—went un-interpreted. Finally and furiously, and in my most assertive sudren girl voice, I said, "Please go downstairs if you want to talk. The rest of us need sleep!"

Silence. It worked…or so I thought, but a few minutes later, the laughter resumed. This time I gave up and decided to battle through their rudeness, as well as the noises made by my bottom bunkmate, a scrawny eighty-year-old pilgrim whose snoring filled the room. I felt lucky that I had made it this far on the Camino without serious snoring issues.

Ironically, it all seemed funny this morning as I rehashed the incident with the young Australian couple who were traveling during their "gap" school year. I marveled at how many countries were represented by the pilgrims I'd met: Japan, Korea, Lapland, even Iceland, and now Australia, as well as the more expected European and North and South American countries. So far I'd not met anyone from the Middle East or Africa.

I packed up, told Doris I'd see her in Acebo, said good-bye to Denis, thanking him for being such an inspiration, and headed out alone—in the snow! Snow in May.

The first village I reached was only five kilometers away, but it took several hours to get there. The café there was rustic and more like a home than a place to get food. There was one large room with a roaring fire at one end (snow in May was maybe not so unusual there), and what appeared to be a family was managing the café. There was a playpen with a baby right in the middle of the room, and several older children and adults of various ages. I would learn later on the path that these were Cathars—members of the ancient religious sect in southern France and northern Spain who had been so brutally persecuted by the Catholic Church of the middle ages. I had long been interested in the Cathars, but I was surprised to learn that there were modern members of the sect. As I warmed by the fire, I took care of myself with water, tea, a banana, chocolate, and nuts. I ran into Harold and Gudrun, who were still astonished that I'd helped them the previous night. Jim, his dad, and their friend came in later.

When I left the café alone, I found the snow falling more dramatically, making visibility along the trail much more difficult. This day would become the scariest of the entire trip. I'd had difficult days, exhausting ones, days when I was sick and unable to walk, but this would be the first time that it was truly frightening on the Camino. I could see no markings. I walked slowly, and wondered if I might really be in danger of losing my way. Eventually I saw a threesome of young pilgrims, two women and a young man, and asked if I could at least walk with them. What is it about a pack of walkers? A pack could just as easily fall over a cliff as a lonely wanderer, and yet somehow there was implied safety in numbers.

They said that they, too, had been unable to find any waymarkers, but we inched along together. They helped me over rocks and mud as though I were an infirm little old lady. Eventually the familiar, yet snow-covered, markers began to emerge, and I decided to move on by myself. We moved through the Pass of Irago, heading toward the highest point on the Camino and the location of the iconic Cruz de Ferro, the Iron Cross. As I headed up the narrow mountain path, the snow that had fallen at first seemed ethereal and mystical, softly covering the leaves and flowers like lace. Clumps of pilgrims passed me, and I in turn passed other pilgrims. We looked like ghostly shrouded figures in the snowfall. This was in fact a beautiful scene, and I wished that my energy was not so focused on staying on the path.

The snow gradually turned to sleet as we climbed, and visibility shrank to only a few feet in front of me. Now there were no stopping places. Climbing higher and higher, I was aware of snow on my eyelashes and on my hair. My gloves were soaking wet when I finally reached the Cruz de Ferro, a towering, weathered metal cross. Pilgrims traditionally placed tokens of hope and symbols of burdens at the foot of cross, but I lingered only a short time here, worrying about the unrelenting snow, the wind, and the freezing temperature. I still had to make my way down this mountain trail before I would reach the road down to Acebo. Even though my guidebook had advised pilgrims to avoid that road (due to its many blind corners, and apparently the poor driving ability of many of the Spanish), I decided to get to the road as soon as I could. At this point, I could no longer see in front of me on the trail.

Aware now that I needed badly to pee, I was relieved when I came upon a small establishment. I guess I could call it that, but in reality what I had come upon was an establishment with no walls! It was a place with an open firepit and a counter with a few items of food for purchase, all of which looked too disgusting to consider purchasing, much less eating. I asked about a toilet. *"Toiletta? Non, non. Latrina,"* as he pointed to the edge of the mountain. How different could a *toiletta* be from a *latrina*? As it turned out, quite different. The rickety structure looked like something from the set of the 1980s *Popeye*—houses perched on the side of a hill and ready to fall to the valley below. I carefully opened the door, and found a dirt floor and a wooden seat suspended over a hole. The hole was in the side of the mountain, and when I peeked down through it I could see the valley below! As I was still seven kilometers from Acebo, uncertain of other places to stop, and with snow steadily coming down, I decided to go for it. I unzipped my pants, pulling them down only far enough to complete the job, and perched above the seat hoping that I would not soon be tumbling down the side of the mountain. Relief was instantaneous, and I was quickly back on the road.

The hardest and coldest part still lay ahead. We were again a struggling little clump of pilgrims, bent over in our efforts to manage the wind and pelting snow. At several points, it was difficult to tell which way to go. For a short while I was walking beside an elderly German lady who, in typical understatement, said, "It's a bit unpleasant today." A bit unpleasant? A bit unpleasant! Seriously.

Eventually we had descended the mountain and headed into the small town of Acebo. I found a café, and, after entering, headed straight for the roaring fireplace draped with hats, jackets, boots, and gloves. I ordered a ham and cheese sandwich and a steaming pot of tea. I found an empty spot at a table and sat, slowly warming and feeling restored. James, his father, and his father's friend entered shortly. They were frozen, wet, and tired, but still wearing the hopeful expressions of the second day of a honeymoon. This was just part of the adventure. I motioned for them to join me.

While eating (they had each ordered a full meal), we talked about our families, their jobs, the law in Brazil, ethics, and our books. They told me that their mom/wife, a lawyer back in Brazil, was holding down the fort, and we all agreed that she needed some serious bling from this trip. We talked the way pilgrims do about visiting each other once we had returned home, with our signed books, of course.

I was aware, yet again, of how many experiences were being packed into each day, and this day was not even over. After walking through the snow on one of the most physically demanding days so far, I was now having the time of my life—with three men!

I had planned to stay put and locate a bed in Acebo, but the men insisted that we push on to Molinaseca, which had been my original destination before the weather had turned bad. I insisted that I needed to stay; they insisted that it would be great to get to Molinaseca. It was not that far away, and they even promised that they would carry me if the walking got too tough. Was

I succumbing to peer pressure at age sixty-five? Yep, I was.

I said that since I walked more slowly, I would start ahead of them on the road, and we'd all regroup for our arrival in Molinaseca. I headed out into the snow and wind, wondering why I had agreed to this, but as I headed downhill, the weather began to clear. By the time I was off the road and onto the marked trail, I saw the most breathtaking valley ahead, decorated with deer, birds, and a sunny, clear sky. It reminded me of that wonderful day that I was on the ancient mystical path all alone...the Camino, one moment horrific and terrifying; a short moment later, sublimely beautiful. I walked alone over the bridge into the charming medieval village of Molinaseca and never did see James, his dad, or their friend. I would not see them again for four days. That was just the way things seemed to happen on the Camino.

Just on the other side of the bridge was a small hotel. For forty euros I had my own heated room with a soaking tub, and for six euros more, my clothes were washed, dried, and folded. High living on the Camino. With just over a week to go, I seemed to be treating myself to periodic hotel accommodations, and I loved it.

After a hot soak and a peaceful nap, I headed into town for dinner. I met Harold and Gudrun, and their German friend, Oskar, at the closest bar. Oskar had been in the *albergue* in Rabanal, and we laughed about the snoring and the laughing Spanish mother and daughter. Oskar, in his mid-thirties, was—like most of the other young pilgrims I had met—trying to figure out his life. He was dealing with the two big issues of adulthood, according to Freud: love and work. I enjoyed these new acquaintances, our lighter conversations, and, most particularly, my solo hotel room.

DAY 22

May 15, 2010

Molinaseca to Villafranca del Bierzo

The medieval church bells woke me at 8:30 a.m. I felt wonderfully rested, ready to go, and even readier as I walked out into glorious sunshine. The distance to Villafranca was over thirty kilometers. I wondered if I could actually make it that far, but that was my plan for the day. We'll see. I was now only ten days from Santiago. The walk to Santiago had seemed to go on for days without any sense of progress, and now Santiago was within spitting distance. I thought about other journeys that seemed to move nowhere in the beginning, and then, as if by magic, the end was suddenly in sight. College had been that way, and my pregnancies, and graduate school. During all those early stages, I routinely forgot how journeys worked, and it seemed I had to relearn the pattern each time.

The beautiful weather, the easy walking (now without a jacket, when yesterday I'd been covered in ice and snow), the end in sight, and my happily rested body made for a wonderful start to the day.

I stopped at a café early in the morning, and it was there that I first spied Matthew. I was not exactly sure when I knew that he was an American, but I was pretty certain he was. It might have been the khaki pants or the baseball cap, or just something about his look. He was older, perhaps mid-seventies, with the kindest face, sparkling blue eyes, and the cap resting on his thinning gray hair. Yep. I was certain he was an American, someone like me, someone from my own tribe.

I approached his table as he sipped coffee, introduced myself, and asked if he was from the States.

"Indeed. I'm Father Matthew from California."

Without editing, I said, "What in the hell are you doing here?"

"I'm a Dominican Friar, and I'm walking the Camino to give thanks for forty years of service to God."

I immediately apologized for my language, and he assured me that it was not a problem. He further explained that due to his work for many years with the Catholic Workers' Movement, he was (and had been for years) on an FBI watch list. He further told me that even today, after so many years, United Airlines was the only airline where he could fly without first being interrogated. It was hard to picture this gentle, older Catholic priest being held in some airport room while FBI agents grilled him. I told him that he was only the fourth American I'd met on the Camino, and he said the same had been true for him. We were both delighted to be with a fellow American. A wave of homesickness stirred in me.

Leaving the café, we latched onto each other and enjoyed the mutual comfort a fellow countryman provided.

We walked over the bridge into the city of Ponferrada, and it seemed that within moments we were talking as if we had known each other for decades. We talked (and walked) non-stop throughout the early morning and into the afternoon. We talked about his work with Mexican immigrants in Mexicali, and how, after his Camino experience, he would be a much nicer person to them, "Because I know how it feels to be traveling and homeless." We talked about the Catholic Church, and my own elusive search for the Big Spirit. We, of course, recounted to each other our experiences so far on the Camino. He told me that he had started the walk dressed in his full ecclesiastical habit as a gesture of kinship with Christ, but that that practice had ended when his sleeping bag, habit, and all of his extra clothes had been shipped back to California. He was down to the clothes on his back, a rain slicker and light jacket (which he had used during the terrible walk in the snow yesterday), a few toiletries, and a change of underwear. I told him about my family, my career, and my thoughts about retirement. This kind of conversation had happened so often and was so predictable that I was no longer amazed. I imagined that I could be a pilgrim wandering pilgrim routes and connecting with total strangers for the rest of my days.

Passing through Ponferrada, we stopped at the massive Templar Castle built in the twelfth century. A fellow pilgrim took our picture standing in front of this iconic structure, my only photo for this day. As we continued walking, we became aware that it was not only a Saturday, but some sort of holiday, as the crowds were growing. We also realized that all this talking and walking had not gotten us to the edge of town where we could pick up the trail. In fact we realized it had been quite some time since we had even seen any waymarkers. In short, we were lost.

Matthew suggested we get a cab to take us to the trail so we could continue the rest of this walk. We neither of us wanted to arrive late in Villafranca on a holiday weekend; and I had already experienced the anxiety of not finding a bed back in Logroño. While in the cab, I managed a phone call to Bill and recounted the last couple of days. Imagine, if you will, that two sixty- and seventy-somethings, essentially strangers, were stuffed in a cab, having gotten themselves totally lost, and the woman of the pair was talking to her husband back in the States telling him that yesterday had been terrifying in the snow, but today was sunny and wonderful, and did he want to speak to her new best friend?

Finally, the cab dropped us off at the edge of town where a group of pilgrims sat relaxing in the grass. They ridiculed us for being in a cab. We tried to explain that our cab ride was our creative solution to being lost.

We walked more silently into the heat of the afternoon and became separated several times due to our different walking rates. At one point when we had reconnected, Matthew told me that he had run into a woman with whom he had walked days earlier. He told me that she was a social worker from Ecuador, and had now picked up her sister at the airport in León. The sisters had planned on walking to Santiago, and he wanted to join them for a stretch. It would be several more days before I ran into Matthew again.

I walked alone for the rest of the afternoon with the sun beaming down. I was certainly not complaining, after weeks of walking in freezing weather. I arrived at the edge of the medieval town of Villafranca around five thirty p.m. and staggered into the village with Maria and her friend, Catherine, the two young Italian women I'd met in Rabanal. They had already checked the *albergues* in this town and had rejected all of them as either too small, too disgusting, or too full. We knew the challenge with arriving late on a Saturday as we scoured the town for lodging. We decided to walk through the entire town until we found a small inn where we'd treat ourselves this evening. Two weeks ago, this much maneuvering at six p.m. would have been unthinkable, but this night I wasn't even concerned. We approached several inns, all of which were full. At the very bottom of a huge hill, Maria asked Catherine and me for our passports and said that she would jog back up the hill and get whatever beds were available, nice or not. We gave her our passports, and, to our amazement, she zoomed back up the hill and disappeared from sight as we slowly trudged up far behind her. We arrived about a half hour later and were thrilled to find that she had secured a bed for each of us and a reserved space on the floor for her sleeping bag. Pilgrims are so nice.

After cleaning up (no hot water in the shower, so only simple face washing and feet soaking), Maria and Catherine headed into the little town square for dinner with other young pilgrims. I walked to the Plaza Major and ate outside at the Restaurante Compostela. I loved this time alone, watching families and other pilgrims and enjoying the golden glow of the sunset as I devoured a pizza. I think my contact with another American today made me long for "American" food.

Earlier, at the *albergue*, I had talked with a woman about the freezing shower, and now saw her eating at the next table with another woman. It dawned on me that these might be the sisters from Ecuador. I went to their table, introduced myself, and learned that they indeed were the sisters from Ecuador. We all shared our fascination with Father Matthew. After dinner, we strolled through the town, getting to know each other. Danielle and Francesca, though sisters, could not have been more different. Danielle was a vegetarian, single, a social worker, and a devout Catholic. Francesca was a married mother of six sons, a meat-eating architect who loved her iPhone, her camera, and her red Spanish wine.

We walked back to the crowded *albergue*, and once more new connections had been forged on this pilgrimage.

DAY 23

May16, 2010

Villafranca del Bierzo to La Faba

There were no musings today—unless you count the beauty of the medieval church, the *albergue* at La Faba, and friendship.

Danielle, Francesca, and I walked out of Villafranca into the Valcarce Valley and along the river. It was cool, lovely, and easy until we got separated after lunch. As I have mentioned, getting separated on the Camino routinely happened, due mostly to the varied walking rate of the pilgrims as opposed to a conscious decision to avoid certain pilgrims. That was what happened today—we were walking at our own dissimilar rates. During the afternoon, I walked alone up into Galicia, and on toward O'Cebreiro. This part of the walk included one of the steepest climbs of the Camino. Based on that information, I had already decided not to go the full thirty kilometers to O'Cebreiro but to stop at La Faba, only twenty-five kilometers away.

I walked ten kilometers alone, lost in my own thoughts. As the steep ascent began, I was walking straight up on woodland paths, shaded, thankfully, but spare of waymarkers. I was pretty sure I was on the correct path, but when walking alone I could quickly get into a panic about direction. Perhaps three kilometers into the ascent, I heard cowbells, which meant cows, which meant a farm, which meant a village must be close, which meant that I was in fact heading in the correct direction. Auditory waymarkers—my first.

At nearly the very steepest part of the climb, I pushed through pine and chestnut trees and into an opening. There before me was one of the loveliest sights of my walk so far—the wonderful *albergue* at La Faba. At five p.m., I arrived. The *albergue* was run by German volunteers, and I was quickly met by a *hospitaleiro* whose only job seemed to be greeting exhausted pilgrims. I went into one of the two structures that housed pilgrims, found a bed, and unpacked. The *albergue* was simple, yet elegant in its simplicity. Pine paneling covered all the walls, and the ceilings had enormous exposed wooden beams. Fresh-cut flowers and a bowl of nuts had been placed on the kitchen table. The whole place was clean, clean, clean. Two more *hospitaleiros* greeted me once I was inside. They made me feel welcome, as if I were coming into their home. Across the courtyard was the ancient stone chapel, Iglesia San Andrés, where a pilgrim priest, dressed in his habit, was preparing to conduct mass. Beyond the *albergue* and chapel were the most stunning, awe-inspiring, and magnificent views of the valley below. This looked like a postcard from the sort of place I would have loved to book for a high-end vacation. I thought that at any moment Julie Andrews would pop up, singing, "The hills are alive with the sound of music!"

I was able to call not only Bill, but also my three boys, the first time I'd heard their voices since I left. I was filled with expansive feelings of love for my family, this beautiful and peaceful place, and the realization that I was just over a week away from Santiago. My low, low points of a week ago were in sharp contrast to the exhilaration I was now feeling. I tried to remind myself of the predictable ebb and flow of life, and to remember not to become stuck for too long in the ebb, and to acknowledge and relish the pleasures of the flow.

After a shower and clothes-washing, I sat in the courtyard, lost in the view. Almost as if on cue, first Danielle and then Francesca arrived, followed by Oskar, then Franz, and, finally, by Harold and Gudrun. We sat into the early evening drinking red wine, eating peanuts, and chatting. We all seemed buoyed by the realization that we were getting closer and closer to the cathedral. The view from the courtyard, the trees, the sounds of birds and cowbells below in the valley, and, finally, the setting sun provided enchantment for all of us. I remembered my lesson of not attaching to perfection, but I could not help but think of this as a most perfect and beautiful evening.

DAY 24

May 17, 2010

La Faba to Hospital de la Condesa

Danielle, Francesca, and I headed out into a glorious, sunny day, and were greeted again with a stunning view of the Valcarce Valley. Danielle immediately caught my attention when she asked if I wanted to hear about the sexual escapade on the Camino. Sexual escapade? On the Camino? Absolutely! Tell me, tell me!

She and her sister had spent the night in the other building at La Faba, and there a couple, on a top bunk, had enjoyed some Camino lovemaking! My sixty-five-year-old brain struggled to make sense of what she was saying. After walking eight to ten hours, most of which seemed to go straight up, how could sex have been on anyone's mind? To say nothing of the the other twenty or so pilgrims in the same room? Had I totally lost my ability to fantasize? "Wait a minute!" I asked, "Did the woman have a mane of curly auburn hair?"

"How did you know?"

"Gudrun and Harold!"

It had to be them. Their sexual energy had permeated the restaurant back in Rabanal. Danielle shared a comment made by another pilgrim, "That was like throwing crumbs in front of a starving man." Indeed.

Danielle and Francesca soon outpaced me as they were walking the twenty-five kilometers all the way to Tricastela. The uphill trajectory dictated another shorter walk for me. I was content to walk alone and soak in the glorious views of the valley. Realizing again that I was only a week away from Santiago, I wanted to savor these last days, especially the beautiful ones. I met an older Frenchman, perhaps in his mid-seventies, who was walking in memory of his wife, who had died the previous November. He told me that he had started walking in April, had walked through France, and was now walking through Spain during this time of his intense grief. Death was alive everywhere on the Camino. This sad, sweet man teared up as he remembered his wife. Once again, I was having a conversation with a total stranger about his deepest feelings. How I wished that somehow we could do this in the "real world," where busyness and accomplishment trumped connection and quiet.

I loved finally being in Galicia, not only because it was the province of Santiago, but because it was also known for the beauty of its lush greenery and its underlying Celtic flavor. When I stopped in the first bar for a rest, just as my guidebooks had predicted, bagpipe music was playing. Homesickness washed over me as I recalled the many times our family had enjoyed listening to recordings of traditional Irish music in our family room.

I arrived in O'Cebreiro, the highest point in Galicia, and one of the highest of the Camino, in early afternoon. I knew this had long been a significant stopping place for pilgrims, and the ancient stone buildings overlooking the valley below added to the drama and reverence. There was, however, an odd disconnect caused by the huge volume of tourists hopping off buses, snapping photographs, and buying up plastic items in the shape of scallop shells and drinking gourds. Tourists on MY CAMINO!

After leaving O'Cebreiro, I met Dorothy from South Africa. She was unlike other pilgrims I had met, as she was a big, crusty woman who cussed and barked about the problems on the Camino. "I hate the bloody snorers! I am bloody homesick. I can't stand these damn *albergues*."

When I asked her why she was here, since she seemed to dislike so much of it, she said, simply and surprisingly, "I was called." I understood immediately. In spite of her coarseness and negative comments, I completely enjoyed walking with her, and did just that for the rest of the day and for a good bit of the following day. We talked nonstop about the political situation in South Africa, the creative ways the country was dealing with its water shortages, and what other countries, including the United States, might learn from them. She told me about the two caesarian sections she'd had in delivering her children. Giving birth was a favorite and familiar topic for Camino mothers. It was as if walking the Camino and experiencing the many emotional births (and deaths) that the Camino had brought had prompted us mothers to each recall bringing our own children into the world.

We eventually made it a few kilometers past Hospital, and there we found an *albergue*. The veranda of the *albergue* provided a welcome spot for rest and enjoyment of the continuing view. However, the veranda turned out to be the only positive aspect of this particular *albergue*. Its single cold and cramped room, lumpy cots, and filthy bathroom were equal to the disappointing accommodations back in Hornillos.

In spite of the accommodations, each of us managed to get a nap, a quick shower, and, later, a Galician dinner (thick stew, roasted meat, and flan) in the small café across the street. Our day ended back in the *albergue* with a rousing visit with the group of young Portuguese men who had joined us in one of the sleeping rooms. These young men, whom we had seen earlier in the day swimming in the river beside the trail, were now walking around in their underwear with their hairy legs. They were charming, funny and delightful. Our big pajama party transformed an evening in a glum *albergue* into a night of laughter and comradeship.

DAY 25

May 18, 2010

Hospital to Samos

Dorothy and I couldn't wait to leave this place. In addition to the deficits I've already listed, we had found both bathroom floors covered in water. After coffee and a tostada, we were on our way.

We fell into a comfortable, similar rhythm. Dorothy was a fast walker like me. The rhythm enabled us to continue our yak, yak, yakking. We'd only met yesterday afternoon, but now words were spilling from of both of us...children, politics, the Camino...

Her plan was to walk the fourteen kilometers to Tricastela and stay there the night. I wanted to walk the additional ten or so kilometers to Samos, inching a bit closer to Santiago.

We arrived in Tricastela at midday, and Dorothy found a place to stay. Her *hospitaleiro* helped me make reservations at Hotel Victoria in Samos. After last night, I had decided to treat myself to private accommodations. I walked the rest of the day without the worry of finding a place to stay when I arrived. The anticipation of another tiny bit of luxury, along with the knowledge that I was only a week away from Santiago (where I would finally see Bill), fed my creeping euphoria.

There seemed to be an undercurrent of this warm feeling as we passed other pilgrims—or perhaps I was just projecting my good mood on everyone.

After our lunch of another huge ham and cheese sandwich (half of which I saved for dinner), I picked up my pack and prepared to leave. Dorothy stood up, gave me a hug and a gift: a small, beaded flag of South Africa she had made. Then, surprisingly, big, crusty Dorothy told me that she had loved walking with me and that she wished me well. I was manifesting something about judgment. *Robin, let go of it.* People's explicit whining and complaining was not necessarily the truth about that person's inner sensibilities. It seemed impossible to get far on the Camino without some sort of lesson.

I walked along wooded paths by the River Oribio, and at one point ran into the young Portuguese men from last night. For most of the afternoon, however, I was walking along the hard asphalt of the highway, always a challenge to both legs and knees. Even so, I enjoyed this solitary afternoon. The sparse markings, and the fact that I kept thinking I was closer than I actually was, made me worry that I was again somehow lost. At one point, I flagged down a cab and asked if I was heading toward Samos. "Si, si. Samos," he said, and pointed in exactly the direction I was walking. Even after so many kilometers of walking, the Camino had not cured my insecurities about getting lost. In my real life, I had relied on two coping strategies to find my way: I had folders with tons of maps and directions to the houses of friends, to stores, schools, and places for meetings; and I had Bill drive me. I felt bad about this, but not bad enough to change.

Here, there was no Bill and no folder chock full of maps and directions. I only had the waymarkers, my guidebook, and scores of helpful pilgrims. Why did I have such trouble trusting my guidebook and myself now?

In late afternoon, after a full day of walking, I arrived in Samos. This was the town with an ancient Benedictine monastery, one of the oldest in Spain and in all of Western Europe. I knew I would go there this evening for Vespers to finally hear the Gregorian chants in honor of my father.

I checked into Hotel Victoria with its nicely appointed rooms and spacious veranda. I sent my clothes down to be laundered and relished what had become a real luxury. After a short rest and shower, I had planned to walk down to the hotel veranda and over to the monastery.

As I walked through the veranda, I saw James from Brazil, his dad, and his dad's friend. The dad looked awful. He was slumped over, his head hanging down, and was near tears. I approached and asked James what was going on. "Oh, he is so homesick, so over the Camino, missing my mom, hating the *albergues*." I totally understood. I hugged them all, but saved my most heartfelt hug for the dad. "I hope it gets better. Hang in there."

I had decided to walk the Camino in part to honor the memory of my mother. My mother had been the stable, consistent nurturer who had not only taken care of my physical needs, but my emotional needs as well. She had taught me how to be a woman, how to be a caring member of a family, and how to nurture friendships. Having fun was also on her list of values. In so many ways she was an amazing, warm, and selfless parent, and I was aware of how much her death had been a challenge for me.

But it was my father who had fed my soul and my imagination, and tonight I would listen to the music he loved and had introduced me to.

How had he fed my soul and imagination? By energetically and relentlessly pursuing his own interests, which were many; and also by explicitly noticing and reinforcing mine.

My father had been interested in so many things that while I was growing up it seemed a challenge to find something he was not interested in. He carved and drew, and took world-class photographs, supplementing his income by taking portraits of children. He was captivated by England, Africa, India and Burma, a love that he instilled in my husband and brother. He loved animals, especially birds; British tweed coats and hats; Italian boots; classical music; fishing; cooking; books; and anything to do with *Wind in the Willows*. He loved that story so much that he named my parents' beach cottage "Mole End" and hand-carved the nameplate that hung above the front-yard fence. He was passionate about Christmas. He was an accomplished tailor and seamster, once making a hat for me to wear to church. And he loved Gregorian chants and ancient and haunting music.

By noticing and being curious about my interests, he nurtured my soul and imagination. He didn't often buy gifts for my brother or for me, but once after learning of my excitement upon hearing *Pictures at an Exhibition* by Mussorgsky, bought me the record for my very own. He also bought for me a record album of Julian Bream playing classical guitar, again after he'd noticed my interest in it. He paid attention to discussions about what I was learning in college, and loved challenging me to think more deeply about my newly acquired information. When I was a young teacher, he visited my class to see a student play; another time he attended an international dinner prepared by my students; and, of course, he took carefully composed photographs of both events. I am sure that if he were alive he'd approve of my pilgrimage. In a way, it was as if he had brought me to the Camino, plopped me down at the starting point, and said, "You need to do this. Life is to be enjoyed and lived fully."

So tonight would be for my dad. I entered the monastery for the evening service where a handsome monk sang Gregorian chants alone. It was a sublime evening.

DAY 26

May 19, 2010

Samos to Sarria

This morning I picked up my clean and folded laundry and began the fifteen-kilometer walk to Sarria. The early part of the day was lovely and cool, the walking flat, and the countryside hauntingly misty. Very Galician. I loved it.

Soon I ran into Danielle and Francesca on the path. At one point, the three of us became lost—very lost—behind a farm. The fact that there were no other pilgrims in sight should have been a clue for us; plus, the small path we were on had become narrower and narrower as we walked along. For a part of the way, the path had been dirt, but now the path was simply the rocks in a muddy stream. We used vines falling from the trees to "swing" our way on the rocks and through the mud. At one point, one of women decided to name our group "The Sorority of Janes," as in Tarzan's Jane, as we swung along the vines in the stream. Jane One, Jane Two, and Jane Three. Why it took us an hour to figure out that we were lost I'm not entirely sure. We retraced our steps, back over rocks and through mud until we arrived at a barn-like structure. Howling dogs were chained up outside. With the help of Danielle's Spanish and directions from the old crone who evidently lived there, we found our way back onto the correct path.

Sarria is famous, only one hundred kilometers from Santiago, and one hundred kilometers of walking was the magic number needed for a pilgrim to receive the much-coveted certificate of completion of the pilgrimage, the *Compostela*. The *Compostela* was awarded in Santiago as proof of the journey and verification of a walker's status as a Camino pilgrim. Consequently, Sarria was a major starting point for many pilgrims who wanted a *Compostela* but who had limited time available to walk the entire route. My guidebook had urged tolerance of the many new pilgrims who suddenly might materialize at this point in the journey. I anticipated huge crowds during the last 100 kilometers and steeled myself for the challenge of finding a bed.

In the late afternoon, we dragged into the city. It did not seem to make a difference that I had been walking for four weeks. At the end of every day, I was spent, and it seemed that the approach to the destination had included the steepest climb of the day. I wondered if life ended that way— with the steepest climb, and the most excruciating steps to get where you needed to go. In the case of life, that climb would be to death.

Danielle and Francesca stopped at the first *albergue* we reached and secured the last two beds. They felt bad about this, but I assured them that I'd find something and that I'd catch up with them in the morning. I was now just an old blasé pilgrim. No bed? No problem. In fact, I found a bed farther up the street at Albergue International, a modern and clean *albergue* that looked more like a sophisticated urban hotel than a place to house pilgrims.

I found a bed on the second floor, the only woman in a room full of men…chatty, funny men who talked about snoring, which they said happened after they got drunk. I begged them to refrain from that much drinking tonight. I showered, washed clothes, and hung them to dry in the designated area on the *albergue's* roof. I then walked into town (more hills) and bought what I guessed would be my last purchases: shampoo, lotion, and snacks. When I returned, I settled down for my afternoon nap. My nap was quickly interrupted by the sound of crying from now the only other woman in the room. I recognized her from earlier on the Camino, and learned her name was Gudrun (another Gudrun) and that she was sick to her stomach, exhausted, and didn't know why she was doing this. She talked, then wailed, then buried her head in her pillow. I knew exactly how she felt, knew exactly what I needed to do, and was loving the notion of being able to pay it forward. When I had taken off on this journey four weeks ago, I had never imagined there would be so much sickness and distress on the Camino.

I told Gudrun I was going to the kitchen to get her a Coke. With lots of hand and facial gestures (gestures that suggested pain and vomiting—I was getting really good at pain and vomiting hand and facial gestures), I managed to get not only Coke for Gudrun, but a bowl of chicken soup! When I arrived back in the room, the men had gathered around her, giving her advice, vitamin C tablets, and, most of all, loving attention. We were our own little hospital unit clucking over our sad chick. Gudrun eventually settled down and managed to eat and drink a bit. I encouraged her to take a day off from walking, just stay here and get better. When I left for dinner, she was fast asleep, and by the next morning she was gone. Things happened like that on the Camino.

I found my way in the *albergue* to the very nice dining room. I had dinner alone and enjoyed the time to think and reflect. I ate properly cooked meat (which was not always the case) with the first ground pepper I'd had since I left home. I ate double helpings of the large, flat green beans, and noted that I was craving vegetables. Sitting next to me was an old couple, at least in their eighties, clearly pilgrims and still wearing their dusty hiking pants and muddy boots. Amazing.

While I ate, I thought about foods I was dying to eat. I wanted vegetables and juicy salads, and steak, and something for breakfast besides tostado. I also thought about all of the slugs and dandelions I had seen on this pilgrimage. I wondered why we Americans thought of dandelions as weeds, and worked like crazy to get rid of them. They were everywhere on the Camino, and were beautiful little yellow flowers. Danielle had told me that in Ecuador, dandelions were revered for the healing power in their leaves, and were often enjoyed in tea. But slugs? That was a different story. They, too, were everywhere on the Camino—huge, black, slimy things the size of small mammals. Most of the woodland paths were covered in slugs that looked dead. Had they not adapted to the dark, moist paths? Or had they been trampled? They hadn't *looked* trampled. What was the point of slugs, anyway? I had never been able to figure that out. This was the sort of meandering my mind undertook when I had no one to talk to.

After dinner, I settled down to sleep, and reflections from my time on the Camino continued to flood my brain. This time, the reflections were not about food or slugs or people, but about the fact that the end was in sight. Being in Sarria meant it was so. With that, I felt an urgency to make sense of this pilgrimage quickly before it was over and all the memories had evaporated. What I didn't yet know was that this experience, these memories and lessons, had been permanently stamped into my soul. They would not only NOT fade, but they would gather strength with the years.

Lying in bed, the idea that occurred to me was related to essence. Long before the Camino, I had been drawn to this notion of the essence of things, and I realized that I searched for it in parts of my life. I loved the essence of things, like the simple, unembellished, handmade wooden furniture of our home. Our one piece of sculpture, a wooden man (whom we called JW after the British artist who carved him), was shaped in the simplest human form with rudimentary features: hollow points for eyes, a small protruding nose over a blank space where a mouth might have been, simple unarticulated arms and legs...JW, our little man.

I had also been drawn to the essence of people, not just things. I continually excavated for their real stories, eager to understand what made them tick. Maybe that was why I had become a counselor.

It occurred to me that I had been reduced to my essence here on the Camino. This essence, this getting to my own core and source, had emerged from two paths, by shedding and by polishing. Spending time, not just a day or a weekend, but enough time away from all familiar parts of my life had enabled this essence to be revealed.

I had shed stuff and things, and also parts of myself. I had gotten rid of my gloves, my mylar blanket, extra food and toiletries that I no longer needed, and now carried only what was essential. Others, like Father Matthew, carried only the barest of things: toiletries and a change of underwear, but no extra clothing. Although I hadn't found scales or a full-length mirror, I was pretty sure that I had also shed pounds. My clothes now hung on me. I had also exchanged flab for muscle, as if I had been reduced closer to my bare bones. I had shed much, or at least shed some, of the parts of my personality that no longer proved beneficial: the need to control the plan for each day, wanting new things to be perfect, or my lack of trust in the face of the unknown. The process of shedding fear and control had allowed room for more hopeful and helpful ways of being, particularly noticing and accepting help along the way.

Essence also arrived through the process of polishing. I felt that I had been rubbed down to my core self through the hardships I had encountered on my pilgrimage: the weather, especially the cold; the daily walking; and the aesthetic affronts of many of the *albergues.* The rubbing and polishing also occurred through the daily managing of unfamiliar surroundings. The kindness and care of others played their part in this process, and I am certainly not suggesting that I became a brightly polished, gleaming pure version of my former self, but I didn't imagine that I would ever think about compassion or perfection or trust in the same way I had before I came to the Camino. I felt I was left with a clearer vision of what mattered in my life. This idea of rubbing or polishing was not like polishing silver to get it shiny and gleaming, but more like the process of the ocean polishing stones with waves and sand and wind until the deep speckles and markings of the stone are revealed.

As I lay in bed that night knowing that I was just one hundred kilometers away from Santiago, I realized that walking the Camino had been the exact choice I had needed to make, the one where I might more fully reflect on my essence. What was this essence, anyway? Was it soul? Or just new self-awareness? Or was it being open to newer aspects of myself and as yet unrevealed ones?

DAY 27

May 20, 2010

Sarria to Portomarin

The walk from Sarria to Portomarin, even with several hills, and the trail filled with new pilgrims, was fairly easy. Arriving in town, I discovered that the first *albergue* was *completo* (full) but I easily found a bed at the next one. I referred to this *albergue*, with its lovely view overlooking the river, as the McPilgrim. It had huge rooms with tons of beds and toilets and showers, massive laundry facilities, and a full breakfast buffet! They had thought of it all, and they were ready for the onslaught of pilgrims, the new and clean ones and the old and ragged ones. There was a slight institutional feel, yet very comforting at the same time. Every conceivable need had been anticipated and planned for.

This whole day had been one of reconnection—with Father Matthew; Danielle and Francesca, my current walking team; but also Dorothy, Doris from Holland, and the entire group from my sad night in Ventosa. It was amazing how we connected, then disconnected, then reconnected, but by now that seemed fairly typical.

After the usual afternoon activities of settling in, Matthew, Danielle, Francesca, and I walked into the town center and to its church, San Nicholas. Matthew was participating in the mass, and both sisters had decided to attend. We all agreed to have dinner together after the service.

I was a little bummed at this plan (I really wanted the day to be over) but I also felt obligated to wait for them. Finally, at eight thirty p.m., they emerged from the church. We found a small place for a fast and cheap meal, but that had entailed (as always when eating with the sisters) much discussion and decision-making regarding the food. Should we get vegetarian? Would it really be vegetarian? Maybe meat would be good at this point? *Make a damn decision and order the damn meal!* Matthew, on the other hand, made quick and easy decisions: chicken, vegetables, and red wine. Check, check, and check!

After dinner, Matthew convinced all of us that we should consider using the services of a *muchilla* (backpack) transport service. These services were quite common, and pilgrims used them to send their packs ahead to the next *albergue*. He also suggested that we make reservations at an inn in the next town. While I loved the idea of having a reservation, and being free from my pack for even one day, I was still uneasy at the thought of being separated from what few belongings I had. The girls ruminated and perseverated about these decisions as much as they had about dinner. Finally, and with Matthew's expert translations, all of us at last had places to stay for the next night. We left our packs at the little shop in the square, and though I felt as if I were abandoning my child to an unknown babysitter, while walking back to the *albergue* I enjoyed a lightness I had not known for weeks, tempered only slightly by my anxiety over never seeing my pack again. My anxiety was not so great that it kept me awake in this sea of strangers back at McPilgrim. In no time, I was out like a light.

DAY 28

May 21, 2010

Portomarin to Palas de Rei

I walked out of McPilgrim, and standing there was Carlos, the *hospitaleiro* from Terradillos de los Templarios, the *albergue* where I'd fainted. Carlos was the wonderful man who had taken such incredible care of me, bringing me soup, a blanket, and the disgusting mineral water I needed to restore myself. And here he was, standing right in front of me. Confused, I asked, "Carlos, what are you doing here? Aren't you still a *hospitaleiro* back in Terradillos?"

"*Non, non. I peregrino!*"

"Wait. What? You are a pilgrim?"

"*Si.Si. I peregrino,*" smiling brightly as he had back at the *albergue.*

I didn't understand. A pilgrim had taken such extraordinary care of me? Just an ordinary pilgrim providing unconditional compassion to a complete stranger? I was left wondering why he had been so good to me. I felt embarrassed, grateful, and amazed by his goodness. Had I manifested such kindness once again to give myself another lesson in compassion? How many lessons about compassion did I still need? We hugged, I thanked him again, we smiled, and were on our way.

The morning was another beautiful, misty, Galician one. I loved the cool, green woodland walking in spite of the slugs. I also loved the break from lugging my pack, even though my shoulders were sore without it. I walked most of the day alone, as Danielle and Francesca were long gone. They did not reappear until after we reached Santiago.

After almost twenty-five kilometers of walking, at four p.m., I reached Palas de Rei, a modern, bustling town. With a couple I'd met earlier, I tried to find my hotel. I was eager to see if my pack had indeed arrived safely. We eventually found the hotel and its manager, who also doubled as the resident bartender.

When his directions to the room failed to make sense, the manager grabbed the couple and me, led us to his car, and directed us to get in. Okey-dokey. He drove us to the rear of the hotel, passing by a table of other relaxing pilgrims. The pilgrims, some of whom I recognized from earlier days, jeered good-naturedly at us for riding in the car. "Please don't tell anyone!" we implored as they snapped photos of us. We all laughed at the scene.

After much fiddling with the key, I was finally in my tiny room and happily reconnected with my pack. I rested, bathed, washed clothes, and headed over to Matthew's hotel. He had already checked in and was showered, dressed, and relaxing over a beer in the hotel bar. We each caught up on our day's hikes, and I offered to buy him dinner, as he'd been so helpful with the *muchilla* transport. He offered to repeat the services—another day of *muchilla* transport and a reservation at the next inn. I wondered if I might be tempting fate to let go of my pack for a second night, but the idea of another day free of my pack combined with a room reservation for the next night convinced me. Last night might have been my very last night in an *albergue*!

Matthew and I went to the hotel restaurant. I was little by little easing back into the world—my old, real world of comfort, staying in a hotel and eating in a nice restaurant. I was anticipating a calm, civilized meal with Matthew, during which we could continue some of our earlier conversations about each of our pilgrimages, the Catholic Church, and our other lives.

Instead, we were joined by another woman with whom Matthew had walked earlier, and whom he'd encountered in the hotel lobby and invited to dinner.

I'm not totally sure why she irritated me so much; probably because it was not the dinner I'd imagined, but also because the woman talked nonstop. Why do people do that, and why does it annoy me so much? It was not only her constant talking, but also what she was actually saying. She said the Camino had been so glorious, every single minute of it. Seriously, EVERY SINGLE MINUTE? She then said that she now stopped each day after only two hours of walking to make the whole experience last longer, that she had not encountered one single problem along the way, and that it was the most amazing thing she had ever done in her life.

While I, too, thought it was amazing, my retelling would certainly be mixed. There absolutely were challenges, disappointments, and problems mixed in with all the great times. Her description seemed disingenuous and it certainly did not ring true with my own experiences.

Whatever the reason, I recognized my crankiness and my exhaustion. As soon as dinner was over, I excused myself, found my way back to my room, and flopped into bed.

DAY 29

Palas de Rei to Ribadiso (almost)

The morning walk on the way to Ribadiso was breezy and warm along sweet-smelling paths— not always the case, as sometimes there were fumes, dust, and foul smells to test a pilgrim. Danielle, Francesca, and Father Matthew were long gone, affording me time alone to ponder what I would miss when this was over. And it would be over in three days! What would I do the first day I didn't walk, and how much would I miss it? And what else would I miss or not miss, for that matter? How different would it be back in my "real life," since the Camino had been my real life for almost four and a half weeks? Here, Santiago was the tether that pulled us along, but back home, there would be no such tether. Except for my few days of sickness, I had walked every single day for these weeks.

I stopped in Melide for lunch and a rest. Still craving fresh vegetables, I ordered an *ensalada mista*—a mixed salad with fresh lettuce, hard-boiled egg, tomato, and pineapple. It was both satisfying and delicious, even with the salt that fell out from the shaker (the top had not been secured!). Afterwards, I felt refreshed and ready for the afternoon walk.

Matthew had made a reservation for me at a small inn just off the N547 highway but not exactly in a discernable town. I was worried that I might easily pass it by so I decided to walk along the highway, where the inn would be more easily seen. The N547 was a busy, loud, and dangerous highway. Walking along a highway was always more challenging, with the traffic, the hard asphalt, and now the intense heat—I had stupidly left my sunscreen in my pack. A sunburn would be the order of the day. As I walked, I continually sought out travel directions from others, reassuring myself that I was heading in the right direction.

I began to feel overheated in spite of the water I was carrying and consuming. Not wanting a repeat of two weeks ago, I found a small bar and went in for shade and rest. As I sat in the bar relaxing, a young man came in that I recognized from earlier on the Camino. I remembered him from that first night in Orisson, and the reason I remembered him was that he, along with the young woman I assumed was his girlfriend, had captured the attention of every pilgrim in the dining hall that night. They had captured our attention because they were almost the most beautiful people we'd ever seen. He was young, perhaps thirty, tall with blond hair, a well-shaped, rugged face and beautiful, straight, white teeth that were revealed as he smiled. She, perhaps in her twenties, was equally as tall, with long, slender legs. Her grace reminded me of a baby deer. She had a perfectly shaped oval face with large, wide-set eyes. She also had a totally shaved head that I had managed to see only a small part of, as it was wrapped in a scarf. I imagined that she was a therapy patient, walking because she had finished her treatment. I was making up a whole narrative about her, her illness, and the young man who was accompanying her on this pilgrimage. The bald head and scarf seemed to highlight her features. The other pilgrims seemed as unable to take their eyes off of them as I was. We love beauty, and we are compelled to appreciate it. I never met them, but a few times early in my walk, our paths had crossed, and wherever they were, people stared. I motioned for him to join me, which he did. I introduced myself, and bypassing all boundaries, asked him, this total stranger, where his girlfriend was.

"Oh, she was not my girlfriend. I wish, oh I really wish that she were. I really liked her, and we had a great time walking together, but she was much younger, and was just not that interested in me." Hard to imagine.

After our talk, we both stood, hugged, wished each other Buen Camino, and were off. I was certain I would miss this kind of exchange. It just didn't happen back in my real life, though now I wished it did.

I headed back onto the unforgiving pavement and into the now broiling sun and continued my walk. As I walked, I began to make out the shape of a figure in the distance walking toward me on the shoulder of the highway. While I couldn't make out exactly who it was, I could see arms waving. I quickened my pace and soon was able to make out that it was Father Matthew! He was practically running in my direction, and we both began calling to each other. As he got closer, I saw that his faithful khaki pants were ripped, one hand was bleeding, and he was holding a pair of broken glasses in his other hand.

"What on earth has happened to you?" I screamed at him.

"I was hit by a bus! Well, not exactly *hit* by a bus, but bumped by. I landed in the field on the side of the road. I'm okay, but my glasses are broken."

Trying to grasp what he was saying, I yelled, "You are seventy-two, for God's sake. You could be in shock!"

He assured me that he was fine, that he could move everything, that the blood on his hand was just a small scrape, and that the biggest issue for him was his broken glasses. He told me that he had passed the inn where my reservations were—it was just ahead—but that he hadn't yet managed to find his own inn. Perhaps he had passed it and now he was backtracking his steps. It was only later that I realized he'd booked our rooms in two separate inns, perhaps because as we were getting closer to Santiago, finding beds was becoming harder and harder.

He continued to assure me that he was fine, and that he wanted to keep walking to find his inn.

We hugged, he took off in the opposite direction, and I headed away on the N547.

In a very short while I saw the sign for my inn. I was so relieved; relieved to soon not be walking, and to again be reunited with my pack. The inn had two small houses used for the storage of packs. The door to the first building was locked, but a note on the door said that the innkeeper was across the highway. Hoping the second building might be opened, and not wanting to cross the busy highway, I walked to it and found it also locked. I sat on its porch in the shade trying to gather my strength and managed to complete a call the *muchilla* transport company just to confirm my pack was here. The clerk assured me that it was, but he wouldn't let me talk to the owner because, "The boss, she is eating and drinking." Eventually, an old woman arrived with keys, and after a round of charades, produced my backpack.

I checked into my charming room in the inn. It had pretty print curtains with matching duvet on the bed and a red-tiled floor. I showered, washed clothes, and went in search of the old woman and the location of the clothesline.

Through much sign language, I learned that the clothes could be hung in back of the inn and that dinner was at seven. The old woman stamped my *credencial*, refused payment for the room (I guessed until the morning), and insisted, against my wishes, that I turn over my passport. My passport had always been checked at the *albergues*, but this was the first time I was required to relinquish it. I felt uneasy about doing this and uneasy about her odd interactions. Something seemed slightly off about her, but I nevertheless handed her my passport.

After taking care of my laundry, I relaxed on the shaded veranda next to the restaurant. Lizards darted back and forth as the sound of the highway traffic droned on. I was soon joined by a mother and daughter from Sweden who were doing a three-day bonding walk to Santiago. As we sipped our chilled white wine, we discussed the issue of my passport. I found my situation a bit more disturbing when they reported that they had not been required to turn theirs over. I decided that after dinner I would confront the old woman and retrieve my passport.

The three of us enjoyed a simple but tasty dinner of roast chicken, vegetables, and a dessert of homemade cheeses with prune marmalade. The dessert was surprisingly elegant for such a rustic place, and I made a mental note to remember to serve prune marmalade (if I could ever find any) with cheeses for a dessert. During the dinner I found that I was the expert, teaching this duo all they needed to know about being a pilgrim, even for three short days. How had that happened? Me, the expert?

After dinner, and with the encouragement of the mother and daughter, I headed out to get my passport back. I noticed that the old woman was now in her small garden patch on the other side of the highway, hoeing and weeding her vegetables. I dashed across the N547, walked over to her garden, and standing as near to her as I dared, said, as politely as I could, "I need my passport, my *passporto*, and if you are worried about not being paid, I'll pay you now." I opened my wallet for her to see my Euros. Her response was unintelligible to me. Gibberish. She then looked blankly at me and returned to her hoeing.

Here is the thing: I am Southern, and a female, and the youngest in my family. I acquiesce. I get along. I am not a confrontational person. That is true, but only partly. I also possess a fairly formidable will, which, under the right circumstances, I have no trouble using. On the eve of my wedding, the only advice my father had for Bill was to beware of my will.

I can only recall two childhood events where my will had prevailed with my father. That was no easy task. I had once begged him to give me a ride on his bike handlebars like my friend's father had done. After Dad finally caved in to me, I had a short, painful ride on the curved, very sharp handlebars of his English bike. That would be the last time I would make such a request.

The second time was on a sweltering August night in our un-air-conditioned house near Virginia Beach, Virginia. Though we lived close to the beach itself, we never ever went swimming after dinner. On this particular night, finding the heat unbearable, I employed every bit of my will to arrange a trip to the beach after dinner. I whined, cajoled, begged, argued, and pleaded, while my sweaty arms repeatedly slid from the table for dramatic effect. To my astonishment, within a short amount of time, my father was frogmarching us to the car to GO TO THE BEACH AFTER DINNER! As we rode in silence, my young girl's brain became aware of two things: First, I was being such a brat and hadn't actually, really expected that we would go. I merely wanted to spread my misery around. Second, tucked away in my mind was the awareness that I had discovered a really formidable tool—MY WILL.

Throughout my life, my will had periodically served me well, whether getting through graduate school or walking these past weeks on the Camino. And now my will was going to get my passport back.

I inched closer to the old woman, and folded my arms across my chest. With my chin thrust out, only inches from her face, staring right into her dark, beady eyes, I said in a loud, authoritative voice, "I *will* have my passport. I am not leaving your yard until I have my passport." I was now fairly shouting. She stared back, hesitated for just a second, then tossed down her hoe and stomped into her house. Within minutes, she returned, waving my blue passport. Thank you.

DAY 30

May 23, 2010

Ribadiso to Arca do Pino

In spite of our standoff in the vegetable patch last night, the old woman was pleasant and chatting as if last night's drama had never occurred—the passport debacle must have been only a dim memory. She was even kind enough to make a reservation for me at a small *pension* in Arca. Since I already had a reservation for my arrival night in Santiago, my days of arriving at my destination at the end of the day hoping I'd be lucky enough to find a bed were over. There would now be a small series of "last things": My last *albergue*, my last full day of walking, my last time carrying my pack, my last ham sandwich, and so on. It was really sinking in. I had actually done this thing. Well, almost. I was, however, carrying my pack again, as there was no Matthew to arrange for the *muchilla* transport. Even so, I liked the feeling of having all of my meager belongings with me.

The Swedish mother and daughter and I left together, but by the time we reached Arzúa, five kilometers away, they had peeled off for a second breakfast! They would learn. Or perhaps not, with only three days of walking. Too much food could be as problematic on the Camino as too little.

I walked on by myself and I seemed to be dragging. I couldn't tell if it was the heat, or the fact that I was again carrying my pack, or that I was just worn out and done, wanting this to be over. There would be no rushing; it would take what it would take. This was the final stage of labor, and the very hardest.

I continued throughout the day, taking breaks for rest and water. The trail was packed with what appeared to be "real" pilgrims trudging along and non-pilgrims out for a Sunday walk in May. Many of the non-pilgrims were singing, skipping along, looking refreshed and happy. For some reason I found myself amazed that they weren't as tired and spent as I was. Their lighthearted mood irritated me. I was cranky, and if Santiago hadn't been just around the corner, I would have happily walked into Arca, put down my pack, and declared my pilgrimage over. Instead, I tried to scoot away from groups of any sort in order to be alone and to reflect.

At the end of this twenty-kilometer walk, I found the *pension* where I would stay tonight. It was a house in a neighborhood. The father of the house and his English-speaking teenage son showed me to my room, pointed out where to hang my laundry, and listed which restaurants in town would be suitable for dinner.

I showered, did my laundry, and realized that this would probably be my last time of washing my sweaty hiking clothes. While rearranging my pack, I realized that I had lost one of my crocs, my elegant little evening wear shoes. How on earth had that happened without my noticing? Even though I knew that Bill would be bringing other sandals, I still had two evenings where I wanted to wear something other than hiking boots. All I needed was a pair of flip-flops. Surely I could find something in the town.

In my bare feet I went to the living room and found the owner's son. I asked where I might find a pair of cheap sandals. "No problem. Wait here." In minutes the father appeared, motioning for me to follow him to the garage. There he handed me a pair of men's flip-flops, size 12. "Oh, no," I shook my head. "Too big." I pointed to my much smaller feet. "Gracias, but I want to BUY sandals!" I shouted for emphasis and pulled out my Baggalini purse, showing him my money. He put the flip-flops directly into my hands and vigorously pointed to my feet. Then he walked to the driver's side of the car and pointed at me and then at the passenger's side of the car. This was all very clear. I got in. This was the second time on the Camino that I was getting into a car with a complete stranger, a man who spoke no English, and somehow I was not freaking out.

In silence, he drove up the street to the third house. He parked, got out, and motioned for me to follow. I clumped up the walk and onto the porch in the size 12 flip-flops. We were greeted there by a smiling, middle-aged woman. We followed her into the house, and then into the garage, except that it wasn't really a garage anymore, but a store of sorts. There were shelves of sunscreen, shampoo, tampons, scarves, and sandals! They both smiled, and waved their hands in the direction of the sandals. I looked over the stock, and found a pair of espadrilles, ladies' size 8. This particular pair was black with gold thread detailing and were slingbacks, unlike any I'd ever seen. I loved them and they fit perfectly. I paid the woman 26 Euros, we all hugged, and headed back to the car. A gift of the small spirit variety.

That evening, I walked into town for dinner in my stylish new espadrilles. I sensed an air of anticipation, not just my own, but with the few other pilgrims that I saw. I ran into the Italian couple I'd met in the awful *albergue* in Hornillos who had been so despondent about the accommodations and the reality of the Camino. Tonight, however, they were walking hand in hand and beaming. She shouted to me from across the street, "*Mañana! Mañana!*" "Yes, yes! *Mañana!*" I shouted back. I was aware of being aware, of wanting to punctuate this evening the way my first night had been punctuated back in St Jean. I wanted to notice and savor every bit.

I loved eating dinner alone. It gave me even more time for reflection and with that was a sense of magic. How had this happened? Really. How had I done it? Starving, I devoured the rich Galician stew, slow-cooked with beef falling off the bone into the rich, oily sauce. As I ate, I retraced each day of my Camino, the people I'd met, the challenges I'd faced, the distress, the funny and serendipitous events. I acknowledged my sadness at not having encountered the Big Spirit…at least not how I'd imagined I would encounter it. I remembered all the encounters with the little spirit, and was grateful for each one and for all the help I'd received along the way. I wanted to remember every single second of tonight and promised to myself to remember every single one that tomorrow would bring. My guidebook had advised to let the last day, the one entering Santiago, be whatever it was. It said I should not try to impose some particular way of being as my pilgrimage came to its end—just note and savor whatever feelings and experiences were presented. All I had to do was pay attention. I could do that.

After dinner, I walked back to the house as the sun was setting. I felt peaceful and full, full of spirit, in touch with something. As I passed the house where I'd gotten my sandals, the lady was sitting in her yard in the cool of the evening. I smiled and waved and kicked up a foot pointing to my sandals. "*Gracias, gracias*. I love them!" I called to her. She waved and smiled.

DAY 31

May 24, 2010

Arca do Pino to Santiago de Compostela

My heart was already pounding before my feet hit the floor. This was it, my last day as a pilgrim. Reflection would happen in the days and weeks ahead, while this day would be for walking the last eighteen kilometers into Santiago.

I packed up for the last time and took my pack into the kitchen area. The father was sitting at the table drinking coffee, and I joined him for coffee and toast. He picked up my pack, and grimaced, *"Muchilla grande!"* *Yes*, I thought; but couldn't imagine what else I might have discarded. I had already gotten rid of my gloves, my crocs, and most of my toiletries. What did it matter now? I was almost done. I liked that he took an interest, and through hand gestures learned that he also had been a pilgrim. Of course he had been a *peregrino*. So much kindness. I knew he understood the significance of this last morning.

We hugged, naturally. I picked up my *muchilla grande* and was off. It was a cool, bright morning, and the walking, through fragrant eucalyptus trees, was flat and easy. I felt oddly detached, wanting it to both be over and yet to go on and on. Throughout the day, I didn't see one other person

I knew among the thick crowds of pilgrims and tourists making their way toward Santiago. I passed over Lavacolla, where ancient pilgrims bathed before entering the city; and then over Monte do Gozo, the Mount of Joy—the elevated place where the cathedral was first visible to pilgrims. Stories of emotionally overwrought pilgrims breaking down at this site were abundant. Leaving it meant that the next big thing would be Santiago.

I was finally at the outskirts of the city, and recalled a conversation with a young Irish woman on my first night in Orisson. She had warned that even though you reached the city, getting to the actual cathedral would take forever. I remembered telling myself that night to avoid her whining negativity, yet as I slogged through the city, her words rang true. It was taking forever to get there. I even had to stop several times to massage my toes and change into dry socks. Along the way, I did run into the young German lawyer from several weeks ago. She was walking from the opposite direction, and had already seen the cathedral. She said, "Oh, you will cry like a baby," and was off. I hadn't wanted to be directed about how I might feel at the cathedral. I was trying hard to stay present and true to whatever the experience might be. Maybe I *would* cry (I was a first-class crier) but maybe I wouldn't. These last moments would unfold as they were supposed to.

And then, almost as if by magic, I was there in the main plaza of the city, a huge courtyard surrounded by a beautiful hotel, government buildings, and this stunning and magnificent cathedral. I just stood as a lump formed in my throat. But no tears. I stood longer, watching as others arrived. I was aware of so many tourists, many more than I had seen on the walk. There were, of course, huge numbers of pilgrims arriving as well. My word for the pilgrims was STRINGY, and I used this as a way to differentiate them from tourists. The pilgrims had stringy hair; stringy, taut muscles; and stringy clothing, faded and worn. They were haggard, sunburned, yet beaming and giddy. Some pilgrims plopped their packs and sticks down and lay on their backs on the pavement, laughing and smiling. The tourists, on the other hand, seemed well-groomed, well-fed, and happy, of course; but they did not display the giddiness the pilgrims did after days and days of walking.

I hardly knew what to do, or what I should be doing. I felt relieved and grateful, and with a sense of unreality. The whole of the arrival was overwhelming yet it also seemed so ordinary. I had similar feelings after giving birth, knowing that something profound had just happened, while also being aware of the simple, ordinary things that surrounded me. I was aware that the experience of simply putting one foot in front of the other, day after day after day, each day arriving at a new and foreign shelter, had been imprinted in me. Now I was aware that from this point on, I was free to do whatever I wanted to do. At that moment in the plaza it just wasn't clear what that might be. I decided to get my picture taken in front of the cathedral and found someone to do that. It was my only picture of this long-awaited moment.

Next I went to the pilgrim's office to get my *Compostela*, my official document of completion. Even though I had been on the hunt for five weeks for a mystical experience, I now really wanted that physical piece of paper! It had been earned through some tough days, and I wanted it. I had always been like that. As a young middle schooler, long past caring about Girl Scouts, once a childhood passion, I became fixated on getting my Curved Bar as I had met all the requirements for that badge. Even though my enthusiasm had waned as I checked off each requirement, I plowed on, and then, upon completion, endlessly bugged my scout leader until she forked over my Curved Bar. It was promptly put away in a drawer as I began to pursue the wonderful work of adolescence.

I joined the snaking line of other pilgrims at the pilgrim's office. I ran into three pilgrims whom I vaguely remembered. One of them said, "You're the woman who helped me find my lost camera one day." The episode was lost to me, but he pulled out his iPhone and scrolled through a massive archive of photos until he found a picture of me. "See. I took your picture after you found my camera." One more connection, even though I was no longer walking.

I eventually reached the clerk, one among many, who was dispensing the documents.

"Did you walk the whole way?"

"Well yes. Well, I mean no. You see I got sick. Well, actually dehydrated. Well, no actually I was sick. More tired than sick. I walked almost 400 miles. But I did walk the last 100 kilometers required to get my *Compostela*. Blah, blah, blah."

She waved her hand as if to say, "Stop. I can't take any more."

She then asked me my name, and I showed her my *credential* with all those stamps. I knew the *Compostela* would have my name inscribed in Latin, yet the clerk seemed puzzled about the translation of "Robin" into Latin. She flipped through a massive book of names and re-flipped. The flipping went on for a while until she finally asked her neighboring clerk for help. The clerk just snapped, "For heaven's sake. Just put ROBIN." She filled in my name in beautiful calligraphy, and handed the *Compostela* to me. "Congratulations." We both smiled. Done and check.

Now that I had taken care of my last official business (except for the pilgrim mass, which I'd attend tomorrow), my attention and energy turned to my husband, who was in flight to Spain at that very minute. I couldn't wait to see Bill and I wanted to greet him in a ceremonial way upon his arrival, in keeping with the spirit of the day. I headed to the hotel to see if they could fix a tray of fruits and cheeses and Spanish ham (!) for him to enjoy when he arrived tomorrow. I figured that he'd be arriving about the same time I would be at the pilgrim's mass, and I wanted him to have a small surprise waiting in the room after five weeks of being alone and two days of travel. The hotel was just across Praza do Obradoiro from the cathedral, and there we had reservations for the following two nights. It was the beautiful Hostal dos Reis Católicos, built in 1499 by Isabella and Ferdinand as a respite for pilgrims, and it was the oldest hotel in the world in constant use. We had decided to treat ourselves to this upscale *parador* for a few nights before taking our driving trip across Spain to Madrid. The hotel was spectacular in every sense: beautiful antiques, massively high ceilings, oriental rugs, artwork beautifully framed, and smooth, dark wood everywhere, worn with age to a glossy chestnut; fresh flowers, exposed stone walls and archways, statues, and carved chairs and doors. By the time we left this hotel, we had ranked it as one of our all-time favorite places.

The concierge was friendly and accommodating, and yes, they would be happy to arrange for a gift platter of cheeses, ham, fruit, and bread for tomorrow afternoon. And yes, they would be happy to include a bottle of bourbon (Bill's favorite). They just needed to check on the price of the bourbon. That bottle would be 120 Euros! Bourbon? In Spain? What was I thinking? I changed the order to two glasses of bourbon.

Once the gift tray order had been taken care of, the clerk asked me where I was staying for the night. I told him that I had reservations for myself at a small inn further away. He then told me that the room we'd booked was also available for tonight if I'd like to avoid relocating tomorrow. I told him that I was certain it would be too expensive. He asked what I was paying at the other inn. Was he trying to make a deal? At Hostal dos Reis Católicos? Was it even thinkable that I had perhaps carried my *muchilla grande* for the very last time? I told him that I was paying 110 Euros. "For a few more Euros, you can stay here tonight, and I will be glad to cancel your other reservations." With that, this wonderful place would be my home for the next three days. No more walking, no more lugging my pack, no more figuring where things were, and not only that, I would be staying in this indescribably beautiful place! I smiled, nodded, and he snapped his fingers to the valet, who picked up my pack and led me to my room.

I entered the room through an intricately carved door. The ceilings were high. I was not good at figuring heights, but maybe ten feet or twenty or even twenty-five feet—high, high, high. The windows were draped in thick burgundy curtains and overlooked the plaza. There was more artwork, lush carpets, scented soaps and shampoo and lotion. And on the king-sized bed were sumptuous linens whose thread count I could not even imagine. I ran my hand over the sheets, just experiencing their cool softness. The contrast to the past five weeks was stark.

I unpacked, arranged my meager belongings, and then soaked in the deep tub for the longest time. I was in total heaven, and aware how quickly I reverted back to comfort. It was not as if I hung out in luxury back in my real life. My upbringing had been frugal. My early married life of raising three sons on one income (Bill's) had also been frugal. It was only after the boys were launched that Bill and I began to enjoy a few luxurious pleasures—travel, decent wine, some artwork. I relished this afternoon in my room.

After my soak, I stretched out on the magnificent sheets and napped a while. Around five p.m., I decided to explore the old part of the city, get some dinner, and hopefully run into some of my pilgrim friends. I dressed for the last time in my Camino wear: my salmon-colored shirt, clean hiking pants, my new espadrilles, gold hoop earrings, and the only makeup I'd worn for five weeks, my lipstick. I felt fixed up, relaxed, and excited about the evening ahead.

As I walked toward the small square that was off the plaza and in the shadow of the cathedral, I told myself that whatever the night brought was what was supposed to be. I wanted to see friends, but if that didn't happen, it would be okay. Last night I had enjoyed the solitude, but tonight I wanted to be celebrating with others. Even though I was trying hard to be mindful of whatever unfolded, I desperately wanted some reconnections. As I walked to a restaurant in the little square, everywhere I looked, I saw celebrating pilgrims. There was screeching, hugging, drinking, laughing, and picture-taking. I wanted to be part of all this jubilation, but it was hard to create alone. I told myself that I would be celebrating, but it would be tomorrow and with Bill.

I found a table in the open square, and ordered an omelet and a glass of red wine. As I was reading the menu, I was aware that someone was standing by me. I looked up and saw Franz! Franz, who had saved my life in Leon…Franz, who had been so instrumental in getting me back on the Camino after I got sick.

"Oh, my God!" I screamed.

"I knew you'd do it," he said laughing. We were both jumping up and down, laughing, hugging, celebrating. It was simply wonderful.

I asked him to join me and tell me everything about the rest of his walk. He seemed more focused on the fact that I had made it. I was a little uncomfortable with so much attention, but so happy to be sharing this night with such a significant person in my pilgrimage.

Shortly Carlos, the lovely *peregrino* who had also helped me when I had been sick, showed up. More screaming, laughing, hugging, and catching up. Franz and Carlos compared notes as to which of them had had the harder time caring for the sick old lady. Carlos acted out the way I looked when I had fainted. Crossed eyes, tongue hanging out, not pretty.

Shortly after Carlos arrived, the two young Italian women from a week ago, Maria and Catherine, also appeared. We were having a full-scale party. We talked into the evening, each of us enjoying these spontaneous and joyful reconnections. After a while Maria and Catherine said that they had to leave. Everyone at the table stood up, and it was clear that Franz would be leaving with the women. Carlos also appeared to be moving on. We all began the long good-bye hugs. When Maria and I hugged, I told her that I knew that she would be okay, and that with some time, the grief for her mother and sister would lessen its grip. We both teared up, and she said that it was because of people like me that she also believed she would get better. In truth, I had spent only a few hours with her, that night in Rabanal as Denis told his story, and then again in Villafranca as we searched for a bed. This was how pilgrims talked. We said good-bye to one another again.

They left and I ate my omelet, not believing this wonderful night. I was thrilled to have been able to again thank two of the people who had been so kind to me when I was sick. As I finished my dinner, I was aware of a commotion several tables away and looked up to see Father Matthew with people grabbing and hugging him as if he were a rock star. I waved my arms, and motioned for him to join me. The only thing that would have made this evening any better would be if Margarite had shown up. Throwing money around like a madwoman, I offered to buy Matthew dinner. We talked for an hour, filling each other in on the last days of our pilgrimages. He told me to be sure to attend the pilgrim mass on the following day, as he'd be one of the celebrants. I invited him to stop by our hotel the following night to meet Bill. The exhaustion of the day and the excitement of this night finally caught up with both of us. We said our good-byes and left for our hotels. Even though I was giddy with the evening fun and with the knowledge that my pilgrimage was over—and that, at long last, I'd be seeing Bill—I had no trouble falling fast asleep.

DAY 32

May 25, 2010

Santiago de Compostela

Today, at long last, was the day Bill would arrive, but first I had to get to the *parador's* noteworthy breakfast buffet. It closed at 10:00 a.m., and it was already 9:45! The cumulative exhaustion, coupled with the peaceful and luxurious accommodations, could have kept me snoozing on and off all day, but I was not going to miss this breakfast. I threw on some pilgrim clothes, brushed my hair, and tore through the maze of halls toward the dining room. It amazed me: For the past five weeks, I had walked across Spain and found my way to wherever I was going, but here, when I walked out of my hotel room, I was totally lost!

With the help of kind strangers and hotel employees, I finally found my way to the dining room. I was just in time.

The buffet was the grandest I'd ever seen. Tables were filled with juices of all sorts: papaya, apple, orange, grapefruit. There were fruit bowls and platters, trays of assorted cheeses and breads of all kinds—croissants, cakes, baguettes, bagels—, more Iberico ham, and sliced sausages of every kind; eggs prepared in any fashion you desire; coffee, tea and other drinks, and so much more. I piled my several plates high, and stuffed myself. I couldn't remember the last time I'd eaten so much. I waved to several other pilgrims who were doing exactly the same thing, some of whom were now dolled up with makeup, painted nails, and real clothes.

After breakfast, I strolled across the plaza to visit the cathedral before the start of the mass. I joined a line of tourists and squeezed under an umbrella of one, as it started to rain. During my pilgrimage, it seemed that the people, the serendipitous events, the natural beauty of Spain, and the search for the elusive Big Spirit had always seemed more transcendent to me than the churches, famous sites, or statues. I was, therefore, very surprised by my reaction and my tears when I finally saw the famous statue and casket of St. James. I prayed again to my mother, prayed for my family, asked for help in not forgetting the many lessons I'd learned, all of which pointed to love, peace, and healing—now my mantra.

It was almost noon, and I made my way into the cathedral for the mass. The sanctuary was packed with hundreds and hundreds of people. I found one of the few available standing spots toward the rear. A middle-school field trip had gathered in this same spot and I found myself between the girls and boys. They had apparently been separated by their chaperones, but even the splendor of the cathedral couldn't tamp down the preteen hormones. Do I need to say any more about that?

I was swept into the energy that permeated the cathedral just before the start of the service. Or was I just keyed up awaiting Bill's arrival? Or both? My heart was pounding, my throat felt dry, and I was aware that I was holding back what felt like a flood of tears. I felt that if I really started crying the tsunami would never end.

The service began, and I was awed by the pageantry and ritual I was observing. I loved seeing the majestic priests, and among them I spied Matthew in his red cassock, looking so different from the disheveled pilgrim he had been several days ago. He was beaming. I loved hearing the reading of the list of countries that represented the pilgrims who were here, and started crying at the mention of "Americanos." When it was time for communion, I couldn't imagine how every single person in this immense cathedral would receive a wafer. To my amazement, the priests fanned out in all directions, and within minutes a wafer was melting in my mouth. I offered thoughts of gratitude as the tears flowed. I was actually taking communion in the Cathedral of Saint James. Me, a girl from Oceana.

And the tears began—a release after so much time away from everything and everyone I knew. It came with the realization that this spectacular but arduous journey was over, with the anticipation of seeing my husband again, and with the majestic and awe-inspiring service. It all poured out of me. I was heaving with tears aware of the mixture of strong emotions welling up inside of me.

After communion, my thoughts turned to Bill. Was he already here? Just yards away in the hotel?

I knew the ritual swinging of the great 500-pound *botafumeiro*, the huge incense burner, would be a sight not to miss, but in all honesty all I could think about was him.

I slipped out of the side door, past the giggling middle schoolers, and ran across the plaza to the hotel.

A brief word about my marriage: It was a real one. In other words, we'd had our fair share of hard times along with all the good ones. We'd had fights over ridiculous and not so ridiculous things; and after almost forty years, we found ourselves still polishing the rough edges off of our relationship. It was wonderfully fun, constant, and challenging all at the same time, but after so many years, we had settled into a mostly comfortable and compatible life together. We shared everything and talked constantly, and if anyone ever said to me that they needed to tell me something in confidence, I always checked: "Okay, but you know that doesn't include Bill." The heart-throbbing giddiness of our early years had evolved into a solid friendship. Simply put, Bill was my best friend. Yet, as I raced across the plaza, with the tears falling in earnest, I felt like I was falling in love for the first time.

I ran inside the hotel and up to the desk clerk.

"Is my husband here yet?"

"Oh *si, si*. He has arrived. He should just be getting to his room."

I flew to the elevator, down the hall, around the maze of hallways that now seemed endless, and finally arrived at our room. I fumbled the key and began pounding on the door, shouting, "It's me! It's me!" (as if it would have been anyone else!)

I could hear Bill padding across the floor. The door finally opened, and I fell into his arms crying, squealing, laughing…"I have missed you so much. I will never, ever leave again!" (Whatever will it be like when one of us dies, which will surely happen?) He was laughing, and I was crying as we hugged for minutes.

When the hugging and crying calmed down, we sat down to enjoy the feast that had been prepared by the hotel—breads, cured meat, various cheeses, fruit, nuts, china plates, linen napkins, an ice bucket, and two glasses of bourbon. Our nonstop chattering went on into the afternoon as we both filled in the details of our lives of the past five weeks.

Around four p.m., Bill's jet lag caught up with him. While he napped, I caught up on the hotel's Internet.

At six p.m., we got ready to explore Santiago and have our dinner. I laid out some clothes—real clothes—that Bill had brought. As I dressed, Bill noted what he called my "four-pack," and indeed, I had muscles everywhere. I could now see my changed body in the hotel mirror. It was wonderful putting on real clothes that now hung on my slimmer, more muscular body.

That night, we strolled through the town enjoying the sights, the energy of celebrating pilgrims, and our first meal together in such a long time. It was a quiet and beautiful evening, and I was relieved beyond measure to be back with my husband. I was looking forward to the prospect of returning to my old life.

After I Came Home

Describing our week of travel across Spain and our return to Alexandria would be fairly straightforward; putting into words the tectonic shift that had occurred within me during my pilgrimage would be far more challenging.

We enjoyed several more days exploring Santiago, luxuriating in the splendor of our hotel, and even meeting Matthew. Bill fixed Matthew's broken glasses while he enjoyed his favorite gin and tonic in our room. Bill also had a chance to meet the sisters from Ecuador and the young lawyer from Germany, but sadly he was not able meet Franz and Carlos, my Camino saviors.

We spent the next week driving across Spain, touring Salamanca, Segovia, and Ávila. Our trip ended after several days in Madrid.

Even though I normally love traveling, in truth I was weary of Spain and of traveling. I hungered for my own bed, kitchen, food, and friends. As thrilling as it was to be reunited with Bill—and it was thrilling—I was also feeling a letdown of sorts...a sadness, a kind of postpartum depression. Not walking just felt strange. Every day for the past weeks had involved a kind of survival. It had been a hard thing, but no one had made me do it. Now I found myself a bit off-kilter and guilty for feeling anything other than pure joy at being reunited with my husband.

We had an uneventful flight home, and slowly reentered our old lives. I sent gift baskets to the two women who had been so instrumental in mentoring me for this journey. I emailed all of my friends from the Camino, and heard from everyone except Franz. I packed away my hiking pants, boots, shirts, hiking stick, hat, and socks, hung up my pack, and threw away my godawful pajamas, happy to never see them again. We took friends to dinner who had so lovingly watched over Bill during my absence. I received flowers and congratulatory notes from our sweet sons. I developed my pictures and placed them in my new Camino album.

I found myself driven with busyness. I assumed that must have been to keep the multitude of feelings at bay. When genuinely curious people asked me about my pilgrimage, I lacked adequate vocabulary to really describe what it was like. I would say that it was hard—harder than I'd anticipated—and yet I didn't want to convey that it was a negative experience, just a difficult one. I would say that I knew it was transformative, but I couldn't say exactly how. I just knew that it was. I could tell them how incredible the people were, and give examples of our fun times or their many kindnesses, but I couldn't find words to tell them that I could have an intimate conversation with a complete stranger, coupled with a sense of deep connection, in an instant—and that that sort of thing didn't happen just every now and then, but almost daily. I could describe my homesickness, the beauty of Spain, the many serendipitous events, the little glimpses of spirit, all of the help and kindness from people whom I would probably never see again; but nothing I said was powerful enough to ensure that my friends really understood.

As happy as I was to be home and to be among the familiar parts of my life, I felt as if I were nowhere. And I was nowhere for a while. I was certainly no longer a pilgrim. Even if I took daily walks, which I usually did, it was not the same. And I definitely was not my old self. I felt that some sort of alchemy had occurred for which I had no words. I found myself reading and then rereading and rereading again my Camino journal, trying to conjure up the magic I had experienced. I spent time looking at my photographs and rereading my guidebooks, trying to understand, to make sense of this simple yet complex thing. This was not like returning from an ordinary trip. I felt as if I had feet in two separate worlds but not planted firmly in either. I was in a liminal place.

Gradually, with the passage of time, I did move back into my old "real" world, and I brought my accumulated learnings with me. With time, my callouses healed, my four-pack gave way to some flab, and some pounds crept back on.

Eventually I was me, only more me than before. I was left with the lessons and the memories, more treasured even than the photos or journal entries or the email addresses of pilgrim friends.

And These Were the Lessons...

Compassion: Early in my pilgrimage, a young German traveler said to me, "Everyone on the Camino notices your pain, and they will try to help if they can." The greatest part of this lesson was learning how to notice. Noticing enabled compassion to be enacted. That night in Logroño, after such a hard and long day, I watched Margarite paying attention to the other pilgrims and finding what she might do to help them. I had thought I understood compassion, but this single event highlighted for me the notion of actively noticing another's situation and needs. The lemon drops and tea given to me for my sore throat; the soup brought by Franz; the man who took me to get my sandals; these were all acts of compassion that began with their noticing of my situation. It seemed as if people were constantly scanning for ways to help. As people showed me compassion, I was then eager to show compassion to others, a great circle of care. I wondered if I would remember this back in my busy suburban life. How could I create more of it? How could I make this central to my life? I felt that *this lesson alone was the greatest one.*

Manifestation. I think of manifestation as my creation of the life I find myself in. In truth, I don't quite actually believe that I am creating every single thing in my life (in spite of all the metaphysical works I have read that say precisely that). It seems there is luck; and there are random events; and there is help from others; and tons of other inexplicable aspects to living. However, during the challenging times on the Camino, it was incredibly helpful and illuminating to ask myself, "Why am I creating this obstacle or challenge right now? What could I learn from this?" Looking through the lens that tells me my life is my own creation helped reduce my feelings of victimhood and provided a nugget of illumination. The challenge became a gift I was giving myself. When I returned home, I remembered this, though not in every single waking moment; but the thought is now lurking in the recesses of my mind, whether I am caught in traffic (Oh, yes. Patience. I get it), or realizing that I can't fix every challenge faced by my kids (Oh, right. Control. That's such a hard one for me).

Essence. Extra weight on the Camino was an impediment to walking. Each night as I packed and unpacked, I surveyed the contents of my pack for items that could be given or thrown away. I became mindful of buying (and therefore carrying) only the few items I would need within a day or two. With this simple physical process, I became more aware of the situations and ideas and habits that also needed inventory, and possibly could be discarded. Discarding the old made room for the new and fresh. Being open to new situations, ideas, and different ways of doing things made the journey more interesting and engaging. I developed a brand-new appreciation for the essence of things.

Perfection. When I became ill on the Camino, I realized that my pilgrimage was not turning out to be the perfect one I'd conceived. I thought the best way to handle that disruption was to abort the trip. Receiving the help and encouragement from Franz to continue, despite the mess, was an important, necessary, and long-overdue lesson for me. While today I still find myself saying things like, "It was just a perfect Christmas," or, "It was a perfect day," or, "That was a perfect meal," I realize that in fact it never is perfect nor could it have been. I am happy to have a new awareness that I can enjoy things that are good and beautiful without the need to seek perfection in them. And with that, I am trying to perfectly accept my own imperfection.

Waymarkers. On the Camino, the yellow scallop shells and arrows pointed the way, and getting lost occurred whenever the waymarkers were overlooked. Some waymarkers were hard to see, though with care and attention they could be found. Help from other pilgrims was also a waymarker for me. Asking for help, or directions, or advice, or support always seemed to result in exactly what was asked for. The challenge was to notice and to be receptive of help in a form that might not have been anticipated. When I was sick and asked the old nun for help with an emergency ticket to Madrid, Franz was the unexpected waymarker who provided the help I needed—help that at first I didn't recognize. Since returning home, I am far more likely to ask for help and to be open and aware of its arrival, even in forms I had not expected.

People. Quite simply, I loved the people I met on the Camino. I found them to be the highlight of the experience. One woman I spoke with after we had returned told me that she had been so busy connecting with the people that she routinely forgot to write in her journal, take photos, or visit any of the sights along the way. It could be argued that people who choose to walk the Camino, leaving behind all things familiar, walking sometimes in extreme conditions, and sleeping in strange places each night, are driven people. The *peregrinos* I met were driven and beckoned in a way that was not logical. They reported that they felt a pull so strong that it could not be ignored—they were compelled to walk the Camino. To be in the company of fellow seekers for five weeks felt like coming home to a family.

Voice. I cannot say that I learned this lesson entirely on the Camino, but I can say that the decision to walk the Camino was a result of paying attention to my own voice. The decision was ultimately not a rational one, and even though it was well-researched and planned, it nonetheless required a leap of faith in the face of the obvious risks and the considerable unknowns. Listening to my own voice and following its urgings resulted in a decision that happily and profoundly informed my life. The lessons of the Camino continue to change my perspectives and understandings of who I am. I'm more than glad that I listened to that voice.

Bill's Email May 24, 2010

Dear Friends and Family,

The Pint-Sized Pilgrim arrived today at the cathedral in Santiago, received her official "compostela," had her picture taken on the steps, and promptly checked into the VERY nice hotel right next door for a "bubble bath major." She has walked 500 miles (actually 400) in 32 days, been frozen, baked, snowed on, sleeted on, rained on, chased by dogs, pee'd in 50 mph winds, fainted, had pilgrim flu for 4 days, made wonderful friends (including an alarming number of boyfriends), and has apparently taught a fair number of Spanish bartenders along the way how to mix monster gin and tonics. She has lost one of her shoes (????) as well as 10 pounds, says she is going to burn her boots, is sunburned and looks like a she-hag, and wants me to bring over the most recent "Veranda," "Town and Country," and "Traditional Home." And another pair of sandals. She said she does not want her walking shoes.

I'm flying to Madrid this afternoon (thank you, Diane, for the ride to IAD) and taking a short hopper immediately to Santiago, where we will sip sangria and people-watch for a couple of days.

Then down to Salamanca for two nights, on to Segovia and Avila, and finally into Madrid for two days. We're flying out and will be home by June 1st. I am sure she will thank each one of you for your comments and well wishes when she is back at 502, and I am equally grateful to you for the calls, drop-bys, emails, and delightful dinners that I have enjoyed in my recent, and now thankfully ended, re-bachelorhood.

Bill

Author's Notes

It goes without saying that this pilgrimage would not have been possible without the complete support and encouragement from my husband, Bill. It would be hard to imagine many husbands who would put up with their wife's total absorption in preparing for a pilgrimage, generously send their sixty-five-year-old wife off for five weeks all alone, endure the upsetting phone and email conversations surrounding her illness and desire to come home, and, finally, provide comments, support, and encouragement in the writing of a book about a Camino pilgrimage. I am truly lucky.

I am also grateful to Laura Potts and Joan Campbell for their help, information, and encouragement in preparing for the pilgrimage. I am grateful to friends and family, especially Thom Blair Jr., for sustaining Bill while I was gone. I am especially grateful to our three amazing sons, Macon, Brooke, and Will, for their love and support, and for not thinking of their mother as an old lady who had completely lost her mind. Thanks also for the loving support of the Blair women, Lee, Tirzah, and Liz.

Many thanks to my editor, Jane Karchmar, for her expert guidance and attention. Also thanks to Haley Chung at Opus Publishing for her patience and creativity in the design of the book. And finally, I am so thankful for all of the assistance and support in the writing of this book. Diane Reukauf and Susan Thompson provided hours of honest assessment throughout this process.

The names of all pilgrims in this book have been changed in order to preserve their identities.

I used the term "*albergue*" throughout the book for consistency. These pilgrim shelters are also referred to as "*refugios*" or "hostels." Some were private, some municipal.

I used the term "*hospitaleiro*" as a generic term for volunteers at the *albergues*, again in an effort to be consistent. These volunteers checked in pilgrims, stamped the *credentials*, sometimes served meals, and helped solve problems and provide support. There were also some who were paid for their services.

A NOTE ABOUT WALKING: The Camino winds through fields, highways, woodland paths, meadows, up mountains, through the *meseta*, and through farms, cities, and villages. Nothing was ever consistent or predictable. The terrain, weather, and walking conditions—urban, rustic, holy, simple, elaborate—all make up the Camino.

Made in the USA
Columbia, SC
12 July 2020